The Complete Guide to Punctuation

A Quick-Reference Deskbook

Margaret Enright Wye

Illustrations by Gloria Ewig Judson

A SPECTRUM BOOK

Prentice-Hall, Inc., Englewood Cliffs, New Jersey 07632

Library of Congress Cataloging in Publication Data

Wye, Margaret Enright.
    The complete guide to punctuation.

    "A Spectrum Book."
    Includes index.
    1. English language—Punctuation.   I. Title.
PE1450.W93 1985   421   84-18021
ISBN 0-13-160292-6
ISBN 0-13-160284-5 (pbk.)

TO GEORGE

10 9 8 7 6 5 4 3 2 1

ISBN 0-13-160292-6

ISBN 0-13-160284-5 {PBK.}

Editorial/production supervision by Elizabeth Torjussen
Cover design © 1984 by Jeannette Jacobs
Manufacturing buyer: Anne P. Armeny

The idea for the illustrations comes from a previously published series of
overhead projection packets on the business letter that the author wrote
with Gail Fann Abbot in 1982, under the auspices of National Instructional Systems,
Inc.; P.O. Box 1177; Huntington Beach, CA 92647.

This book is available at a special discount when ordered in
bulk quantities. Contact Prentice-Hall, Inc., General
Publishing Division, Special Sales, Englewood Cliffs, N.J. 07632.

Prentice-Hall International, Inc., *London*
Prentice-Hall of Australia Pty. Limited, *Sydney*
Prentice-Hall Canada Inc., *Toronto*
Prentice-Hall of India Private Limited, *New Delhi*
Prentice-Hall of Japan, Inc., *Tokyo*
Prentice-Hall of Southeast Asia Pte. Ltd., *Singapore*
Whitehall Books Limited, *Wellington, New Zealand*
Editora Prentice-Hall do Brasil Ltda., *Rio de Janeiro*
Prentice-Hall Hispanoamericana, S.A., *Mexico*

Contents

Preface

Today's business communicators are unanimous in their desire for a traditional back-to-basics review of American punctuation practice; that is, a rule-by-rule approach to the marks of punctuation used in this country to communicate a writer's mental direction to a reader.

This book has been designed to address concerns about standard business punctuation practices and to build confidence in applying punctuation rules, as well as to meet the needs of the business communicator in designing and writing business letters. The workbook approach is essential because it introduces a set of related rules and applies those rules immediately so that the communicator will have first-hand knowledge of success.

The average person's concern about punctuation is mainly with commas; this book has been designed to address these concerns first. Each rule concerning the use of the comma is presented and the concept is then reinforced immediately by a Rule Practice. Concept and practice are then reinforced again by the Additional Exercises found in Section 5.

Section 2 is a brief overview of grammar rules that supplement the punctuation discussion. Section 4 has been included as a resource. Many times I have wished for just such a compilation of abbreviations. The stories used to emphasize a punctuation or grammatical point in the book are just that—stories that I've either read or heard during my career and that I have recast for the occasion. The stories may not be entirely accurate (at this writing I have read three different versions of the Winston Churchill story about prepositions), but each story has been extremely useful in illuminating the spirit of the problem under discussion.

As you use the book, please note any difficulties you may encounter. If you like, pass on your comments to me: P.O. Box 3277, Manhattan Beach, CA 90266.

Immediately following this introduction is a Diagnostic Test that can be self-administered. It is designed to direct the reader to problem areas in punctuation covered in the book. The headings in the exercise correspond to headings in the book. After completing the test, go to the area most in need of clarification. Good luck!

DIAGNOSTIC TEST

Punctuate the following sentences. The only mark of punctuation that has been provided is the period at the end of each sentence. There are 50 sentences, each worth 2 points.

Commas

1. Johnson is a responsible fair-minded manager.
2. In adding the receipts Fred made a serious mistake.
3. If you have any questions Ms. Smith the personnel department bulletin may be able to answer them.
4. The credit union will stay open late on Wednesday Thursday and Friday of next week.
5. Mr. Hickson carefully locked the safe but he forgot the combination.
6. Mrs. Tyson on the other hand never forgets a thing.
7. The company does not withhold federal or state income taxes from your checks.
8. The first speaker is Thomas B. Redding Ph.D. and he will keynote the conference on Thursday morning.

Semicolons and Colons

There are some commas needed in these sentences also.

9. Tom Simmons simply quoted the closing figures he did not comment on their validity.
10. Our company is initiating a new four-day week however the participation is flexible and begins at 6 30 A.M.
11. The conference has been held in Denver Colorado Palm Springs California and Salt Lake City Utah.
12. The following names were on the promotion list namely Elliot James Valerie Drummond and Kent Butler.
13. These names were left out of the recent telephone directory please add them to your list.
14. The people in accounting will be working Saturdays for the whole month furthermore the people in accounts receivable will be working overtime next month.
15. Mr. Kelly will attend all the meetings Ms. Ward on the other hand will attend only the first meeting.

Dashes, Parentheses, and Hyphens

Commas are needed also.

16. There is only one thing on John Smother's mind profit.
17. Hammers nails saws these are the tools of the trade.
18. There were over thirty three applicants for one position.
19. The answer to that question is in the management book see Chapter 2 page 24.
20. John Doe hereby agrees to pay the undersigned four hundred and twenty five dollars $425.
21. Alec Parsons has lost the figures figures that were needed to close the bid.
22. (Punctuate for emphasis) The three competing offices San Mateo Santa Rosa and San Francisco have been setting district sales records.

Quotation Marks

Remember to punctuate for identification.

23. The success of the company said Mr. Allerton is due to the combined efforts of management and staff.
24. Did you hear Mr. Lopez say No one is willing to work hard any more.
25. There is only one area that will give you the opportunity to exercise your talent said Dr. Jordan.
26. When did you hear from him last asked the manager.
27. Mr. Browning the district manager used these exact words Be completely honest and success is inevitable.
28. What is the new manager's name asked the foreman.
29. Doris Moore suggested Tom Ward had the right idea when he asked What's in it for me during last Friday's staff meeting.
30. Seeing the approaching truck Janice shouted Watch out.

Apostrophes

Add 's or ' and any other necessary punctuation.

31. Mr. Jones talent for cost accounting cant be duplicated in this company.

32. The word success has two cs and two ss.
33. The Board of Directors meeting has been postponed.
34. There will be five minutes delay before the presentation begins.
35. The Wallaces warehouse is on the next block that warehouse is the Adamses.
36. Tom and Daves study is better than ours.
37. Did you hear about Hendly Incs sale?
38. Its a pleasure when its gearshift works.

Numbers

Underline any error in number representation.

39. Invoice No. 4,276 has been delayed for 3 days.
40. Approximately two-thirds of the vote went in our favor.
41. The final shipment will include fourteen desk blotters, 2 new Selectric typewriters, and 24 hand calculators.
42. Be sure to stay on Highway Fifteen for at least twenty-five minutes before looking for the exit.
43. 5 new accounts have added to the staff in the past fifteen days.

Capitalization

Underline any problem with capitalization that you see.

44. Please meet mr. thompson at his office monday.
45. The Audience enjoyed brunch on fine China after the morning Lecture.
46. We celebrate the signing of the declaration of independence on july 4 each year.
47. The Jones Brothers construction Company is remodeling both the Woolworth and the Smiley Buildings.
48. While in night School, i'm studying French and Shorthand.
49. While you're at the Drugstore, please pick up a box of Kleenex and a Bic Pen for me.
50. Last Wednesday, Mr. fox returned to Culver city.

For correct punctuation, see Key Section, at the back of the book.

THE COMMUNICATION PIPELINE

(Punctuation says something.)

1

Punctuation Rules

USING COMMAS

The most frequently used mark of punctuation is the comma. Basically, commas are used to enclose and to separate.

To Enclose

Rule 1: Use commas to set off nonrestrictive clauses or phrases. (Nonrestrictive means unnecessary, added information.)

A. A clause is a group of related words that has a subject/verb core.* A nonrestrictive clause can be either an adjective or an adverb clause.

1. An adjective clause is a subject/verb core word group used to modify a noun or pronoun and is introduced by one of the following relative pronouns:

   WHO, WHOM, WHICH

   Mary, whom you just met, is my friend.

*See Section 2, The Sentence.

1

Mary, who is my friend, just left.

This car, which broke down recently, is not worth selling.

2. An adverb clause is a subject/verb core word group used to modify an adjective, verb, or another adverb and introduced by one of the following:

after	if	until
although	in order to	when
as	provided	whenever
as if	since	where
as though	so that	wherever
because	than	whether
before	though	while

We decided, after we thought you had left, to go home.

We paid the check, although we had not enjoyed the meal, and departed.

You must, whether you like it or not, attend the meeting.

B. Use commas to enclose phrases that interrupt the flow of the sentence. A phrase is a group of related words that does not have a subject/verb core.

Tom stood there, his damp face glowing, and told us he had just run five miles.

The bicycle wheel, obviously bent out of shape, had to be replaced.

Susan, in order to save time, rode her bike to the store.

C. A parenthetical expression is a word, a phrase, or even a clause that can safely be deleted from the sentence without changing the meaning of the sentence. Here are a few expressions that are often used parenthetically:

as a consequence	I believe	nevertheless
as a result	if necessary	of course
as a rule	in addition	on the contrary
as well as ____	in brief	on the other hand
as you know	in fact	therefore
for example	I understand	to be sure
however	moreover	we all agreed

Your plan, I believe, should be adopted.

Mary, however, may not go.

We can, I understand, use Kathleen's office.

D. A noun in direct address is either the proper name or a salutation used when speaking directly to someone or something. (Note: the word in direct address is *never* of grammatical importance in the sentence.)

David, will you please close the door.*

May I help you, sir?

We will give you, Mr. Jones, one complimentary copy.

*See Section 2, Sentence Analysis.

E. An appositive is a noun or noun substitute that immediately follows another noun and renames or identifies the first noun. When the appositive is nonrestrictive, it must be set off by commas.

My friend Suzanne visited my office yesterday. (I have more than one friend, so the name is important.)

Suzanne, <u>my friend</u>, visited my office yesterday. (There is a prejudice in this language in that information following a name is usually considered to be nonrestrictive.)

The television program originated from Washington, <u>our nation's capital</u>.

F. An abbreviation that follows a name (either personal or company) to indicate a title, degree, or legal standing is always set off by commas.*

Johnson & Johnson, <u>Ltd.</u>, is having a sale this week.

Thomas M. Cromwell, <u>M.D.</u>, has given up his practice.

G. "Of-phrases" that follow a person's name and give the location of a firm or residence are set off by commas.

Dorothy Moore, <u>of Seattle</u>, will be here tomorrow to conduct the audit.

William Baker, <u>of Roxwell, Roth, and Assoc.</u>, has given us excellent advice.

PRACTICE COMMA RULE 1

Punctuate the following sentences by applying the rules concerning commas that enclose nonrestrictive elements. In the space provided, indicate the sub-rule(s) being employed by the appropriate letter.

1. The new house as a consequence cannot be sold for six months. 1. _____

2. If you change your mind Harry please call. 2. _____

3. The front window obviously broken was of little use. 3. _____

4. We were all given although we did not know the reason the day off next Monday. 4. _____

5. We had a meeting with Thomas B. Harding of Washington last week. 5. _____

6. We hired Joseph Deerling Ph.D. as a consultant last June. 6. _____

7. I visited Mary whom you have never met last weekend. 7. _____

8. Mr. Smith our treasurer read the quarterly report at the annual stockholders' meeting. 8. _____

*Abbreviated titles are listed alphabetically in Section 4.

9. The new drapes we all agreed were worth the long wait. 9. _____

10. March Bros. Inc. has just opened a new office in our building. 10. _____

11. Many people as you know have come forward to offer Jane help and encouragement. 11. _____

12. You will find Mr. Smith that your account has been adjusted and your balance corrected. 12. _____

13. The Agony and the Ecstasy which was written by Irving Stone is a novel about Michelangelo. 13. _____

14. Speaking to Janet Perkins of Smith & Co. has caused Mr. Homes to change his mind about the merger. 14. _____

15. Aunt Sis a very distant but dear relative is still one of my favorite people. 15. _____

LAST WILL & TESTAMENT
I, George Laslow, leave my entire estate of $15,000 to be divided among my three nephews:
Harold W. Laslow,
Gerald H. Laslow and
William P. Laslow.

Harold W. Laslow obtained an attorney to represent him in his efforts to obtain $7,500 (half of the said amount) because he alleged that, since there was no comma before the _and_, it should be ascertained that the last two names represented one unit.

He won the case, and the judge awarded him half the stated sum.

4

To Separate

Commas are used to separate as well as to enclose. This section encompasses the rules concerning separating sentence elements.

Rule 2: Always place a comma before the final coordinate conjunction in a series. The most common coordinate conjunctions used in a series are <u>and</u>, <u>or</u>, and <u>but</u>. The items may be words, phrases, or clauses of equal rank. The commas are used to distinguish one item from another and to indicate equality within the items themselves.

I want to see you on <u>Monday</u>, <u>Wednesday</u>, or <u>Friday</u> of next week. (Nouns in a series.)

Mary is <u>beautiful</u>, <u>vivacious</u>, and <u>charming</u>. (Adjectives in a series.)

Tom looked <u>under the desk</u>, <u>on the chair</u>, and <u>in the file cabinet</u> for the missing papers. (Phrases in a series.)

<u>Louise wrote the copy</u>, <u>Jim edited it</u>, but <u>John typed the final draft</u>. (Clauses in a series.)

The Stationery Store sells <u>envelopes</u>, <u>folders</u>, <u>labels</u>, <u>etc.</u> at a 40 percent discount. (Never use <u>and</u> plus <u>etc.</u>, as <u>et cetera</u> means "and others.")

Compare:

The store sells <u>stationery goods</u>, <u>envelopes</u>, <u>folders</u>, <u>labels</u>, <u>etc.</u>, at a 40 percent discount. (Here the items in series are also nonrestrictive appositives and could be punctuated: The store sells stationery, goods—envelopes, folders, labels, etc.—at a 40 percent discount.)

The candidates for the position are all either <u>too young</u> or <u>too old</u>, <u>too short</u> or <u>too tall</u>, <u>too big</u> or <u>too little</u>. (The coordinate conjunctions are used within the items in the series.)

With Coordinate Adjectives

Coordinate adjectives are adjectives that come before a noun and are seen to be of equal value; therefore, they must be separated by a comma. Two tests can be used to determine coordination:

1. If the adjectives can be reversed and the description still makes sense, the adjectives are considered to be coordinate and a comma must be inserted.

2. If the coordinate conjunction <u>and</u> can be placed between the adjectives, consider the adjectives coordinate and insert a comma.

The large, sturdy table (We could say <u>sturdy</u>, <u>large</u> table or <u>large</u> and <u>sturdy</u> table.)

The old oak table (Apply the test. These clearly are not coordinate adjectives.)

The pretty small table versus the pretty, small table

(*Notice:* <u>Pretty</u> can be either an adverb describing the relative smallness of the table or an adjective describing the appearance of the table. Here the placing of the comma communicates the writer's choice to the reader.)

Is it a pretty, small table,
or a pretty small table?

With Repeated Adjectives

Sometimes adjectives or nouns may be repeated for emphasis and need to be separated by commas.

It is a <u>long</u>, <u>long</u> road that we have traveled.
All I ever do is <u>work</u>, <u>work</u>, <u>work</u>.

PRACTICE COMMA RULE 2

Punctuate the following sentences by inserting the commas where needed.

1. The vice-president spoke about personnel changes improved equipment and revised production schedules.
2. A simple error-proof method for incorporating the Wang equipment into your organization is enclosed.
3. Endeavor to make your letter concise specific and clear.

4. The local drugstore sells office supplies paper clips pencils pens etc.* that we use on a daily basis.

5. This dress is old old old.

6. Watkins is looking for a permanent challenging secure position with a local bank.

7. The stationery store specializes in diplomas certificates memo pads etc. for school or office.

8. Interviews will be held at 10:00 A.M. 1:30 P.M. and 3:00 P.M.

9. These forms may be used to record the sale of stocks mortgages and other securities.

10. Kathy looked under the table on the shelf and in the desk for the book.

11. The chair is made of wood and leather has a firm texture and is well suited to your office needs.

12. The new extensions assigned to the office are 7264 7265 and 7266.

13. When you come home from the conference I want you to do the dishes fold the clothes and make the beds.

14. In recent months Bob has sold his house bought a new car and moved into a bachelor apartment.

15. The booklet tells you why where and how modern office procedures developed.

Rule 3: Use a comma to separate independent clauses joined by one of the following coordinate conjunctions:

and, or, but, for, nor, so, yet

The important thing to remember is to make sure that the coordinate conjunction is coordinating independent clauses and not some other sentence elements.

Joyce went to visit her mother, but she did not stay long.

Joyce went to visit her mother but did not stay long.

The first sentence has two independent subject/verb cores; the second sentence has one subject and two coordinate verbs and is, therefore, a simple sentence.†

PRACTICE COMMA RULE 3

Identify the subject/verb cores in the following sentences by underlining each verb twice and each subject once; then punctuate according to Rule 3.

*The asterisks in the Practice Rules here and on subsequent pages refer the reader to the corresponding key in the Key Section starting on page 119.
†See Section 2, Sentence Analysis.

Example: <u>Mary</u> <u><u>sings</u></u> in the choir, but <u>John</u> only <u><u>listens</u></u>.

1. The dictionary employs a uniform system of marking yet people sometimes have trouble pronouncing certain words.
2. John has decided not to attend the convention nor will he help organize any pre-convention activities.
3. We discussed the matter with Ms. Shipley and Mr. Lester and they have promised to have the material delivered by March 15.
4. I have decided to stay late today so you may take the afternoon off.
5. We are shipping the material immediately and you may expect it within a week or ten days.
6. You need to make a payment by the tenth of the month or you will have to pay a penalty again.
7. John has promised to fill out the enclosed form and mail it to us by Friday.*
8. Ms. Drake expects to receive the new catalogs from the printer today and will mail you a copy within the week.
9. The canvass was made in the neighborhood of Oak Avenue Elm Avenue Pine Avenue and Walnut Avenue and the results were predictable.
10. We steadfastly maintain our innocence for we are the oldest and most reputable real estate brokerage firm in the South Bay area.
11. A Southern California Edison crew is working hard to repair the damage and we hope to have your power restored by 3:30 P.M. today.
12. This vacation package allows you to enjoy Italy Germany and France in a series of little trips or you can choose one country and enjoy its attractions fully.*
13. Our responsibility was called into question so we could take no further action.
14. We thought the investigation was closed yet we ordered a thorough study of processes materials and prices.
15. It is always better to specify the exact time of arrival so there can be no uncertainty.

Rule 4: Introductory elements are usually followed by a comma.

A. An introductory adverb clause is said to be <u>transposed</u> because the normal placement for an adverb clause is at the end of a sentence. Adverb clauses that occur at the end of a sentence are considered restrictive more often than not.

Mary will be at the meeting if she feels better by tomorrow.

If she feels better by tomorrow, Mary will be at the meeting.

B. Transitional phrases, interjections, or independent prepositional expressions of more than five words are also followed by a comma.

In fact, the organization is involved in an expansion program. (A transitional phrase is a group of words used to relate one sentence to another.)

Gosh, I almost didn't make the meeting. (An interjection is a word used to denote strong feelings or sudden emotions; when followed by an exclamation point, it is considered to be an independent expression.)

At the bottom of the drawer under some other papers, John found the missing file. (Prepositional Phrase)

There are, however, two exceptions to the rule concerning a prepositional phrase of five or more words.

1. Do not use a comma if the introductory prepositional phrase is followed by a verb and the subject of the sentence.

At the bottom of the drawer under some other papers is the missing file.

2. Use a comma to avoid confusion with words that can be easily misread.

In the morning, light filtered through the office window.

C. An introductory verbal phrase that is used as a modifier should be followed by a comma. The phrase can be either an infinitive (to + root verb = to walk, to talk, etc.) or a participle (verb form ending in either -ed or -ing = walked, talked, walking, talking).

While walking to school, Janet lost her wallet.

Perplexed, she looked everywhere for it.

To find her wallet, she had to walk all the way home.

Be particularly careful of the dangling verbal phrase. A verbal phrase is said to dangle when the noun modified is incapable of performing the action described.

While walking to school, a wallet was lost.
(The wallet was not walking anywhere.)

To find her wallet, the long walk home was begun.
(The wallet would be found by a person, not a walk.)

D. Sometimes a noun can be placed before a participle to form a nominative absolute construction. Such a construction is set off from the rest of the sentence by a comma.

The work having been completed, Mr. Jones decided to treat himself to a small vacation.

9

The door being locked, we climbed in through the window.

The question having already been answered, the manager could not understand the delay.

The nominative absolute, then, is a noun immediately followed by a participle and forming a unit of a dependent nature rather than an independent subject/verb core.

PRACTICE COMMA RULE 4

Punctuate the following sentences by inserting the commas where necessary.

1. In making his selection the manager interviewed three different applicants for the position.
2. As I previously told you the meeting will take place a week from this Friday.
3. Because the money has not been appropriated by Congress the program is being shut down.
4. To accommodate my boss I took my vacation in July.
5. The work being already underway it was impossible not to sustain a loss.
6. Wow I just found out I'm going to be promoted.
7. On the other hand it could be that the new comptroller just needs to relax a bit.
8. Having spent several years with that company Tom feels he's now an expert in hydrolic engineering.
9. In the pocket of the purse at the bottom of the basket was $1,000.
10. On Friday we will meet the new manager.
11. Surprised by the interruption Mr. Sellers tried to act noncommittal.
12. As every person who applied was unacceptable Mr. March is running the ad for another week.
13. Before long day seems like night if you are living in Alaska.
14. If taxes have to be increased before the end of the year the country will certainly suffer.
15. Since no one else seems willing I will come in on Friday to do the proofreading.

Rule 5: Certain contrasting expressions are set off by commas:

A. Expressions that begin with not, never, or seldom.

The celebration will be in May, not April.

The conference usually lasts until 5:00 P.M., seldom later.

B. Questions appended to preceding statements.

You did make the appointment for Monday, <u>didn't you</u>?

C. Identical verbs in a sentence.

Most people who <u>go</u>, <u>go</u> early.

D. Clauses built on contrast.

The longer I thought about it, the more determined I became.

PRACTICE COMMA RULE 5

Punctuate the following sentences:

1. The longer I worked the more confident I became.
2. Ted Baxter is the president of E.M.I. isn't he?
3. The weekly sales meeting usually runs for a full two hours seldom longer.
4. Most people who vote vote out of concern for the democratic processes.
5. Although majestic Pikes Peak is more inspiring to look at than to climb.
6. To promote sales campaigns should be developed with the user in mind.
7. The longer Mr. Jones waited the more irritated he became.
8. The fall sale will be held November 19 not November 20.
9. John is going to the conference is he not?
10. In Susan Harris has found a secretary who is dependable imaginative and capable.
11. The longer the meeting lasted the more heated the discussion became.
12. The people who will work work long and hard.
13. You're going to the conference aren't you?
14. Management sometimes works on Saturday.
15. To increase our sales staff and management alike must make a concerted effort.

Rule 6: Certain commas are used for identification purposes.

A. The identification of quoted material involves attribution, or naming the source of the direct quotation (he or she <u>said</u>, <u>inquired</u>, <u>suggested</u>, <u>observed</u>, <u>replied</u>, <u>stated</u>, etc.).

<u>The manager said</u>, "The office staff deserves special recognition for outstanding service."

11

"Bill," called Ralph, "come here!"

Bill called, "Ralph, come here!"

"The office staff," said the manager," deserves special recognition for outstanding service."

"The office staff deserves special recognition for outstanding service," said the manager.

However, an indirect quotation needs no punctuation: The manager said that the office staff deserves special recognition.

1. Commas and periods always go inside the closing quotation marks.

2. Semicolons and colons always go outside closing quotation marks.

3. Dashes, exclamation points, and question marks can go either inside or outside the closing quotation marks.

> Did he ask, "Will you go?" (Both attribution and quoted material are questions.)
>
> He asked, "Will you go?" (Only the quotation is a question.)
>
> "Will you go?" he asked. (The question mark goes with the quoted material, but the attribution is not capitalized as a separate sentence.)
>
> Did he ask you for a "date"? (The attribution, not the quotation, is a question.)

B. Chapter reference, page references, etc. are also used for identification purposes.

> I refer to the material in Volume 10, Chapter 2, page 89.

C. Commas are used to identify the omission of important words.

> Mr. Sellers has agreed to contribute the building; Mr. Brown, the money; and Ms. Kingsley, the publicity.

PRACTICE COMMA RULE 6

Punctuate the following sentences:

1. The proposal stated Further testing of the product is necessary.
2. Tell no one about the proposed merger the vice-president cautioned even though you might be tempted to do so.
3. The first-place winner will receive $1,000; second place $700; and third place $500.
4. The salesman replied The word processor is essential for the office of the future.
5. You will find the cited material in Chapter 4 page 47; Chapter 8 page 107; and Chapter 12 page 272.
6. The president implied that the company was interested in a merger.

7. Competition is what makes used-car sales a challenge concluded the sales manager.

8. Mr. Wallis said Individual interviews are a necessary part of placement.

9. The Exalon Company is proud of its reputation the letter said and we expect our customers to be equally satisfied.

10. I have here the shop foreman retorted facts and figures that prove your report is wrong.

11. The manager asked Is anybody in charge here

12. Did the manager ask Is anybody in charge here

13. Did the manager ask about who was "responsible"

14. Last week Ms. Kingsley made three important personnel changes; this week two more.

15. The manager said The staff deserves special recognition; however, nothing further seemed to be done.*

Rule 7: The punctuation of dates, addresses, and count numbers deserves special mention.

A. Use commas to separate items in an address when the address is written in-line.

Compare:

Mary Jane Furman
427 Benton Blvd.
Kansas City, MO 64124

The invoice was mailed to Mary Jane Furman, 427 Benton Blvd, Kansas City, MO 64124, on Monday. (Simply put: the commas come at the end of every line of a standard letter address.) There is a choice at present between writing out Missouri or using the ZIP code designation in-line, but the abbreviation, Mo., is no longer considered acceptable.

B. Use commas to separate items in a date.

The meeting will be held on Tuesday, January 12, 1982, in the lawyer's office.

Without the day of the month, the comma is unnecessary (January 1982).

The military has had an impact with its practice of writing a date in the form: 12 January 1982.

C. Count numbers of more than three figures are separated by commas. However, identification numbers are never separated. (Invoice No. 4783 does not necessarily mean that there are 4,782 previous invoices.)

1,754,252
872,483

Special usage:

D. Use a comma to follow the complimentary close of a letter. (Only the first word is capitalized.)

Sincerely,
Yours truly,
Truly yours,

E. Use a comma to separate and identify the parts of an inverted proper name. (This is particularly important for those who have two first or two last names.)

Smith, Bert = Bert Smith
Thomas, John = John Thomas

PRACTICE COMMA RULE 7

Punctuate the following sentences and identify the appropriate sub-rule(s) being employed by writing the appropriate letter in the space provided:
   A. Items in an address
   B. Items in a date
   C. Count number versus identification number

Part A

1. There were 7583 people at the conference in Fort Worth.   1. _____

2. The merchandise you ordered on February 9 1982 was shipped to Evergreen, Ltd. 279 W. Olympic Blvd. Gig Harbor WA 90266 on February 10.   2. _____

3. We will be looking forward to the meeting on Thursday May 9 1982 at the Ramada Inn.   3. _____

4. We shipped Invoice 7256 on July 7 1982.   4. _____

5. On March 11 1979 the telephone company celebrated its fifteenth anniversary.   5. _____

6. Mark C. Bloom is located at 1117 Western Ave. Los Angeles California.   6. _____

7. If all goes well our vacation will begin on May 17 1982 and will not end until August 3 1982.   7. _____

8. The company has purchased the old Wheatfield Building at 472 Longview Costa Mesa California.   8. _____

9. There were more than 1473 participants in the audience for the March 3 1982 Association presentation.   9. _____

10. The meeting will be held in May 1983 not March 1983.

10. _____

Part B

Punctuate these to indicate the inverted proper name:
Smith Thomas
Ulack Joyce
Speed Patricia
Holmes John
Wise Buyonne

Part C

Respectfully
Respectfully yours
Sincerely
Yours truly
Regards

Legend has it that the Czarina of Russia saw a note on the desk of Alexander II.

"Pardon impossible; to be sent to Siberia."
She changed the punctuation.
"Pardon; impossible to be sent to Siberia."

USING SEMICOLONS AND COLONS

Rule 1: A semicolon is used to separate independent clauses <u>not joined</u> by a comma and a coordinate conjunction.

> Dr. Tolbert was educated at Harvard; his degree is in economics.
>
> Answer every question on the application form; no space should be left blank.
>
> John will attend the conference; Mary may decide not to go.

The case of the conjunctive adverb and the transitional phrase deserves special attention. The joining of independent clauses is still accomplished by the semicolon:

> John will attend the conference; <u>however</u>, Mary may decide not to go.   (Conjunctive adverb)
>
> John will attend the conference; Mary, <u>however</u>, may decide not to go.   (Parenthetical expression)
>
> John will attend the conference; Mary may, <u>however</u>, decide not to go.   (Parenthetical expression)
>
> John will attend the conference; Mary may decide, <u>however</u>, not to go.   (Parenthetical expression)
>
> John will attend the conference; Mary may decide not to go, <u>however</u>. (Parenthetical expression)

Notice that however is essentially parenthetical and may appear anywhere in the sentence, but it is always set off by commas. When it appears right after the semicolon, it is termed a <u>conjunctive adverb</u> to designate its position in the sentence only. The same may be said for the parenthetical expression that becomes a <u>transitional expression</u> when it appears next to the semicolon.

> John will attend the conference; <u>on the other hand</u>, Mary may decide not to go. (Transitional expression)
>
> John will attend the conference; Mary, <u>on the other hand</u>, may decide not to go. (Parenthetical expression)

Here is a listing of expressions used in these positions:

accordingly,	hence	on the other hand,
actually,	however,	on the whole,
also	in addition,	otherwise,
as a result,	in other words,	still
besides,	moreover,	that is,
consequently,	next	that way,
first	on the contrary,	then
for example,	furthermore,	thus

Note: A comma generally follows such an expression except after a word of one syllable.

Rule 2: A semicolon can be a mark of elevation in some cases.

A. A semicolon separates coordinate clauses joined by a coordinate conjunction when at least one of the clauses contains additional commas. (Optional)

> Mary, who is my supervisor, decided to go; and we had a good time at the meeting.

My supervisor decided a report was needed; and I was assigned the task for this month, for the six-month report, and for the fiscal year-end report.

B. A semicolon is used between items in a series when commas appear within the items.

The conference speakers were Mary Knowles, of the University of Kansas; John Irving, of the University of Washington; and Clifford Speaks, of the University of Southern California.

Rule 3: Use a semicolon to precede such words as for example (e.g., exempli gratia), that is (i.e., id est), and namely when used to introduce examples or illustrations.

Only three people were promoted; namely, Susan Reese, John Towers, and Rex Sunday.

PRACTICE SEMICOLON RULES

Punctuate the following by inserting semicolons where needed. Indicate the reason for your choice in the appropriate space.
- A. To separate independent clauses
- B. As a mark of elevation
- C. To introduce examples or illustrations

1. The allowable discounts are suggested in the enclosed brochure i.e. 20 to 30 percent of all discontinued stock.

1. *_____

2. Mr. Jones you have ignored our polite reminder regarding your overdue account actually this is not the first time you have done this.

2. _____

3. Pete Lundy's itinerary includes San Diego California Portland Oregon and Seattle Washington.

3. _____

4. Please let us know your decision immediately we'd like to begin the sales campaign as soon as possible.

4. _____

5. The first edition went into print two years ago the second edition will be out in three months.

5. _____

6. Several items need to be examined more carefully for example cost-accounting procedures and the year-end report.

6. _____

7. I suppose it's better to work until 5:00 P.M. every day still I'm always ready to go home by 4:00 P.M.

7. _____

8. Renee will program the computer while Carole checks the previous printout that way the problem will be solved more quickly.

8. _____

9. People fear that the word processor will cost them jobs it was never designed to reduce the labor force.

9. _____

10. Mary resembles her father Debbie looks like her mother.

10. _____

11. The new plants will be located on the outskirts of Dallas Texas Phoenix Arizona and Tulsa Oklahoma.

11. _____

12. The decision to move the office which had been in the same location for twenty years was made suddenly but the overall result has been beneficial.

12. *_____

13. The office manager is responsible for all the equipment namely desks typewriters and calculators.

13. _____

14. These statistics were excluded in the first draft please add them to your present edition.

14. _____

15. Both individuals come with excellent recommendations however we can hire only one engineer.

15. _____

Rule 4: A colon is used after a formal introduction that includes (or suggests) words such as the following.

(*Note:* Words such as namely, for example, etc., are never used after a colon.)

The assignments are as follows: letters 1, 7, and 9.

The introduction may be followed by an indented list.

The shipping department has back-ordered these items:
Walnut desk
Umbrella stand
Table lamp

The introduction may be followed by an appositive or descriptive words.

John has one preoccupation: his car.

The introduction may be followed by a long (usually more than three sentences) direct quotation.

Rule 5: A colon can be used to separate two main clauses when the second clause amplifies or explains the first.

There is one major advantage to an IRA account: You don't pay taxes on the amount deposited.

Special usage:

The colon is used after the salutation of a letter.

Dear Dr. Smith:

The Right Honorable Judge Hovermyer:

A colon is used to separate hours from minutes when recording time.

The meeting is to be held at 10:45 this morning.

PRACTICE COLON RULES

Punctuate the following by inserting colons where needed. Indicate your choice in the appropriate space.
- A. After a formal introduction
- B. To separate two main clauses
- C. Special Usage

1. The plane leaves LAX at 4 15 this afternoon.   1. _____

2. Please buy the following at the stationer's
   note pads
   paper clips
   desk calendars   2. _____

3. The manager had only one recourse to fire the secretary.   3. _____

4. The letter served its purpose It saved the account.   4. _____

5. Remember this A fool and his money are soon parted.   5. _____

6. This accounting procedure has two advantages It reduces errors and saves money.   6. _____

7. The office was exactly what we wanted affordable, yet large.   7. _____

8. The meeting has been changed from 1 30 to 3 45 this afternoon.   8. _____

9. Dear Mr. Sellers   9. _____

10. Mark Twain wrote "A powerful agent is the right word. Whenever we come upon one of those intensely right words in a book or a newspaper the resulting effect is physical as well as spiritual, and electrically prompt."   10. _____

11. Ms. Davis recently ordered the following furniture for her new office three desks six chairs two sofas two IBM Selectrics one calculator and one adding machine.   11. _____

12. Our new advertising campaign will be directed towards economy car buyers It will stress mileage maintenance and reliability.   12. _____

13. The sales meeting begins at 9 30 and usually lasts until 11 00 each Tuesday.   13. _____

14. The office uses several different kinds of typewriters IBM Olivetti Olympia.   14. _____

15. Dear Mr Postmaster General   15. _____

DASHES (—) AND HYPHENS (-)

Rule 1: A dash, which is a mark of emphasis, is formed when typing by two hyphens --. The dash makes reading easier.

A. A dash can be used instead of commas for any emphatic, nonrestrictive phrase or clause.

> The business, as you know, is making money.
> The business—as you know—is making money.
>
> My boss, whom you have never met, is in Europe.
> My boss—whom you have never met—is in Europe.
>
> The policy, of course, is still in effect.
> The policy—of course—is still in effect.

Note: A dash can also be used for restrictive clauses that the author chooses to emphasize: The script—that you rejected—has just grossed over a million dollars.

B. A dash can be used instead of a semicolon when followed by words such as <u>namely</u>, <u>for</u> <u>example</u>, etc.

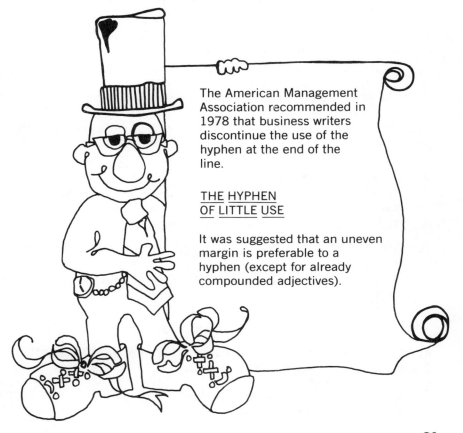

The American Management Association recommended in 1978 that business writers discontinue the use of the hyphen at the end of the line.

<u>THE</u> <u>HYPHEN</u>
<u>OF</u> <u>LITTLE</u> <u>USE</u>

It was suggested that an uneven margin is preferable to a hyphen (except for already compounded adjectives).

The office is in need of supplies—namely, pencils, staples, and paper clips.

That copier has serious problems—in other words, the firm has no intention of purchasing one.

C. If the nonrestrictive element already has internal commas, use dashes to set the element off. (If the dashes are too emphatic, use parentheses instead.)

The three competing firms—Ajax, Lionel, and Fox—were requested to give estimates of the cost.

D. A dash is used instead of a colon to emphasize words.

All Felix Samonal thinks about is one thing—money.

Rule 2: A dash is used to sum up a preceding list or to indicate an abrupt change of direction in thought.

A. The words <u>these</u>, <u>they</u>, <u>all</u>, <u>each</u>, <u>only</u>, etc. are usually used to sum up a preceding series.

Terry Kelly, Bill Smith, and Carol Turner—<u>each</u> of them has access to the storeroom.

B. Use a dash to show an abrupt break in thought, to set off an afterthought, or to show hesitation.

Many executives in this organization have been employed—but you already know their personal histories.

The banquet was held—let me see—was it on a Friday?

Rule 3: Dashes are used in the restatement of certain emphatic phrases.

A. Use a dash for a word that has been repeated.

Shirley Thompson has the folder—the folder she claimed had been lost.

Tom Bright is a slow typist—painfully slow.

B. Use a dash for words that restate or amplify important concepts.

Right now—at this very moment—the decision about the project is being made.

PRACTICE DASH RULES

Punctuate the following sentences for emphasis and indicate the reason for your choice in the space provided.
A. The emphatic dash
B. Summary or change of direction
C. Repetition or restatement

22

1. This course of action as our accountant maintains will save the company a half-million dollars a year.

1. _____

2. The manager has only one goal retirement.

2. _____

3. Experience qualifications and excellent references all are essential to getting a good job.

3. _____

4. Every manager and you're no exception is responsible for a department's budget.

4. _____

5. Mr. Baysworth requested the information information needed to complete the quarterly report.

5. _____

6. We already have branch offices in several states Texas Oregon Washington and Nevada that are operating at a loss.

6. _____

7. The problem is simply solved for example personnel evaluations need to be updated.

7. _____

8. If there are any problems phone no come in as soon as possible to discuss your tax situation.

8. _____

9. Labor equipment and time those are the major concerns in remodeling.

9. _____

10. The experience difficult and painful as it may be should prove profitable.

10. _____

11. Thanksgiving Christmas New Year's these are the only official company holidays.

11. _____

12. Additional road equipment a bulldozer a backhoe and a grader was needed to complete the contract.

12. _____

13. We expect perhaps oh about a 15 percent reduction in staff this year.

13. _____

14. Negotiations after reaching an impasse on June 10 were resumed on July 1.

14. _____

15. Our sales overall sales have increased by 15 percent since the end of the fiscal year.

15. _____

A hyphen is formed by one mark -. It is used to compound an adjective.

Rule 4: A compound adjective consists of two or more words that function as a unit and express a single thought. The compound adjective appears before the noun or in the subject complement position and uses one or more hyphens to join the words.

BEFORE THE NOUN	ELSEWHERE
quiet-spoken man	A man who speaks quietly (adjective clause)

off-the-record comment	The comment is <u>off of the record</u> (prepositional phrase)
government-owned lands	These lands are <u>owned by the government</u>. (verb plus preposition)
high-grade ore	The ore is <u>graded high</u>. (verb phrase)
three-year commitment	A commitment for <u>three years</u> (prepositional phrase)
a 55-mile-per-hour speed limit	A speed limit <u>of 55 miles per hour</u> (prepositional phrase)
accident-prone person	The person is <u>prone to having accidents</u>. (verb phrase)
law-abiding citizen	The citizen <u>abides by the law</u>. (verb plus preposition)
high-ranking official	The official was <u>ranked</u> quite <u>high</u>. (verb phrase)
a <u>well-known</u> executive	The executive is <u>well known</u> (verb phrase)

Exceptions to the rule:
These words are always hyphenated:

1. Numbers that are compounded from <u>twenty-one</u> to <u>ninety-nine</u>.

2. Fractions that function as adjectives: two-thirds majority. (*Note:* Two thirds of the membership agreed.)

3. Words with the prefixes <u>self</u>, <u>all</u>, <u>ex</u>, or <u>great</u>, or the suffix <u>elect</u>. (Selfish, selfsame, and selfless are never hyphenated)

governor-elect	self-respect	great-aunt
all-powerful	self-esteem	ex-President

4. Words that change meaning with the hyphens

re-form (to form again)	versus	reform (to make better)
re-cover (to cover again)	versus	recover (to get back)
re-mark (to mark again)	versus	remark (to notice)

5. Hyphenated words that appear in the subject complement position.

The citizen is law-abiding	The person is accident-prone
The official was high-ranking	The ore is high-grade

You may also use compound adjectives in a series.

All two-, four-, and six-year contracts are to be renewed.

PRACTICE HYPHEN RULES

Punctuate the following sentences.

1. Inspection will begin on ten twenty and thirty story buildings the first of next month.
2. These forms should be filled in by Monday.
3. The filled in forms should be returned by Monday.
4. Three fourths of this year's profits has already been reinvested.
5. A three fourths majority is needed to reinvest the money.
6. The selfish manager considered himself to be self made.
7. This store carries the finest quality goods.
8. This is only a three year contract.
9. The contract lasts only three years.
10. Thomas Coswell is a well known public speaker.
11. The ex football player is now in the insurance business.
12. This business was started by my great grandfather.
13. A certain well known executive has changed jobs four times in a five year period.
14. This building offers one three and five year lease options.

PARENTHESES AND BRACKETS

Rule 1: Parentheses are used to set off and de-emphasize a parenthetical, nonrestrictive phrase or clause. Expressions that are neither grammatically nor logically essential to the main thought of the sentence may range in length from a single word to several sentences. The first word or letter written in parentheses is capitalized only if it is always capitalized.

A parenthetical expression that falls at the end of a sentence is not punctuated as a separate sentence.

> The information is in Chapter 2 (see page 48).
> The item was priced too high ($19.98).
> Please forward the material the usual way (c.o.d.).

A parenthetical expression that appears within the first of two clauses is punctuated as part of that clause.

> The information (see page 48) is in Chapter 2; the answers are at the back of the book.
> If you go early (6:30 P.M.), you may get a place.

You go early (by 6:30 P.M.), and I'll catch up with you.

We need these supplies (we're almost out): pencils, pens, notebook pads, and staples.

He ordered the needed supplies last week (or so he claims); for example, pens, pencils, and notebook pads.

The reply was prompt (within two days); however, no payment has been received.

He was in the office last week (was it Friday?), but I did not see him.

When the parenthetical expression is a question or an exclamation, the appropriate mark is enclosed within the parentheses.

Mr. Ragus wore Jordache (?) jeans to work only once.

We have not met for over five long (that seems too long!) years.

Parenthetical expressions that are complete sentences are punctuated as such.

He did not attempt to answer.   (He could not.)

He did not attempt to answer.   (How could he?)

He did not attempt to answer.   (He dare not!)

The test for parentheses is whether the words of a sentence make sense without them.

Rule 2: Use parentheses to enclose numbers or letters that identify items in a series or list that appear <u>in-line</u>.

> To secure an interview, you must (1) submit an application, (2) provide two references, and (3) pass the entrance exam.

Rule 3: In legal and business correspondence the dollar amounts can be spelled out and immediately followed by the typed numbers (enclosed in parentheses).

> I, the undersigned, agree to pay four hundred fifty dollars ($450) a month to John R. Floyd for the next twelve months in return for the lease of his equipment.

Rule 4: Use brackets to identify words added to a direct quotation of another as well as for information purposes.

The use of [<u>sic</u>] identifies a mistake in a direct quotation (*sic* means "thus").

> "I would sooner go to jail then [*sic*] have to pay." (The correct word here would be <u>than</u>.)

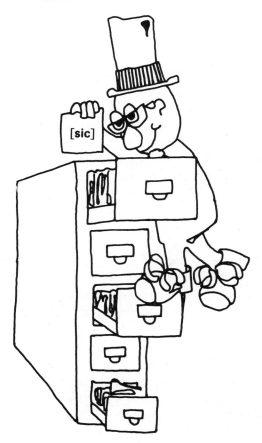

Brackets at the end of a quotation give added information.

> She replied, "I never met Mr. Norman in my life, *to the best of my knowledge.*" [Emphasis added.] (The writer added the italics.)

Bibliographic references appear in brackets.

> Magazines concerned with food preparation are in the habit of sending people all over the world in search of interesting material. [See *Gourmet,* May 1981]

Rule 5: Brackets are also used as substitute parentheses when appearing inside existing parentheses.

> William Butler Yeats was a great playwright. (Some historians [see page 107] suggest that he was a better poet.)

PRACTICE PARENTHESES RULES

Punctuate the following by paying particular attention to the setting off of nonessential elements by the use of parentheses.

1. Management has already embarked upon cost-saving budget reduction see attached supplement.
2. This sale it's our going-out-of-business sale is too good to miss.
3. The department meeting served to 1 improve communication 2 increase quality standards and 3 develop rapport between management and staff.
4. There is no possibility ? that the budget will be approved as written.
5. The normal fee for our service totals seven hundred dollars $700 payable by check or VISA.
6. Our representative Mr. Paul Sloane didn't you meet him at the Atlanta Conference? will be stopping by your office next Monday.
7. The Licensee hereby agrees to pay Licensor on the first day of each month commencing on the first of January Nineteen hundred eighty-three the sum of five hundred dollars $500.
8. (Punctuate a separate sentence) Please compare our product with others on the market. This month's issue of <u>Newsweek</u> has several excellent ads.
9. The assistant director I believe his name is John Thornton* has not returned my calls.
10. The United Nations has several objectives A world understanding B world communication and C world peace.
11. You have already learned see Chapter 1 that financing for this project is dependent on government approval.

Italics

Babbitt
by Sinclair Lewis

*Beyond
Bureaucracy*
by Warren Bennis

*The Organization
Man*
by W. H. Whyte

*The Atlantic
Monthly*

" "

"The Catbird Seat"
by James Thurber

"Chicago"
by Carl Sandburg

"Quality"
by John Galsworthy

"Labor" by Thomas Carlyle

12. We need the representative if he ever gets here to answer our questions.

13. If you follow my suggestion and you should you will reconsider your decision.

14. Go by yourself you can do it on company time and I will sign the authorization.

15. This price was high $1975 but worth it.

QUOTATION MARKS, ELLIPSES, AND ASTERISKS

Rule 1: Direct quotations, the exact words used by a writer or a speaker, are placed within quotation marks.

Direct quotation:

> Our production manager Donna Watson said, "I see a steady decline in production costs as the economy cools."
>
> "I see a steady decline in production costs," said Donna Watson, our production manager, "as the economy cools."
>
> "I see a steady decline in production costs as the economy cools," said Donna Watson, our production manager.
>
> Did Donna Watson say, "I see a steady decline in production costs as the economy cools"?
>
> Donna Watson asked the general manager, "Do you see a steady decline in production costs as the economy cools?"
>
> Donna Watson shouted, "Shut down the machines!"
>
> "Shut down the machines!" shouted the production manager, Donna Watson.

Indirect quotation:

> Donna Watson, our production manager, said that she sees a steady decline in production costs as the economy cools.
>
> Did you hear Donna Watson, our production manager, say that she foresees a steady decline in production costs as the economy cools?

A quote within a quote:

Sometimes it is necessary to quote someone who in turn is quoting a third source.

> Donna Watson said, "I spoke to the general manager, Tom Little, who confirmed, 'There is no overtime available this month.'"
>
> Donna Watson said, "I spoke to the general manager, Tom Little, who asked, 'Is there any overtime available this month?'"
>
> Donna Watson asked, "Have you spoken to the general manager, Tom Little, about 'available overtime'?"

PRACTICE QUOTATION MARKS RULE 1

1. Maria Huffner said We anticipate a 3 percent return of merchandise.

2. A 3 percent return of merchandise said Maria Huffner is anticipated.

3. Maria Huffner said that a 3 percent return of merchandise is anticipated.

5. The report stated According to Maria Huffner A 3 percent return of merchandise is anticipated.

6. Dr. Roger Wilson predicted that the economy will begin to stabilize by next year.

7. The economy suggested Dr. Roger Wilson will begin to stabilize by next year.

8. The economy will begin to stabilize by next year suggested Dr. Roger Wilson.

9. Dr. Roger Wilson suggested the economy will begin to stabilize by next year.

10. The newspaper article stated According to Dr. Roger Wilson The economy will begin to stabilize by next year.

11. The newspaper predicts that it will be impossible to meet the deadline.

12. The newspaper quoted a <u>Newsweek</u> article by the Secretary of State It will be impossible to meet the deadline.

13. The Secretary of State suggested It will be impossible to meet the deadline.

14. It will be impossible said the Secretary of State to meet the deadline.

15. It will be impossible to meet the deadline said the Secretary of State.

Rule 2: Titles of various literary works as well as names can appear in italics (underlined when typed or written out) or in quotation marks. The division is between major (large) works and minor (small) works.

ITALICS	QUOTATIONS
Novels/Books	*Short stories/Essays*
Free to Choose, by Milton and Rose Friedman	"The Discrepancy Between Business and Aesthetic Values," essay by Robert Wilson
The French Lieutenant's Woman by John Fowles	"A Rose for Emily," short story by William Faulkner
Magazines	*Articles*
Time Newsweek	"The Oriental of Bangkok" "Economic Outlook Dim"
Newspapers	*Songs*
Los Angeles Times *The Wall Street Journal*	"If I Were a Rich Man"

ITALICS	QUOTATIONS
Novels/Books	*Short stories/Essays*
Epic	*Poems*
The Odyssey	"Jabberwocky"
Ships	*Boats*
Queen Mary	"Blue Heaven"

Rule 3: A technical word or unusual phrase can be emphasized or clarified by the use of quotation marks. (Usually, these same expressions are shown in italics when they appear in print.)

> The first characteristic to be considered is the "selectivity," the ability of a material to separate salts from water of the membrane.

> The word "distillation" here actually refers to partial distillation wherein heat is applied only until separation begins.

Technical terms should not be quoted in a text addressed to the informed reader; i.e., someone already familiar with the specific technical language employed.

Rule 4: An ellipsis is a series of three periods indicating an intentional omission within quoted material.

Omission <u>within</u> sentence (. . .)

> The sign reads "Violators will be towed . . . cars will be released upon payment of a $50 fine."

Omission at the <u>end</u> of a sentence (. . . .)

> Sears guarantees "All repairs that do not come under the warranty will be made at less than 30 percent of the regular cost. . . ."

Rule 5: A series of three asterisks can be used in the middle of a page to signal that one or more paragraphs have been omitted from a text. (This rule is given for information purposes only.)

    *   *   *

Rule 6: The single asterisk (*) directs the reader to one of three possible places: (1) the bottom of the page, (2) the end of the chapter, or (3) a special section at the end of the book. (This rule is given for information purposes only.)

PRACTICE QUOTATION MARKS AND ELLIPSES RULES

Part A

Underline or put into quotation marks the following expressions:

Faith of Our Fathers (address by John Foster Dulles)

Area Production of Principle Crops (report)

Who's Who in America 1980

The Yearbook of Labor Statistics

The American Commonwealth (book) by Viscount James Bryce

The Crisis of the Old Order (book) by Arthur N. Schlesinger, Jr.

Wealth of Nations (book) by Adam Smith

All systems are go

The Theory of the Leisure Class (book) by Thorstein Veblen

Part B

Use ellipses in the following:

1. There were at least ten executives attending the conference: Allen P. Havier   John Hershey.
2. Successive quotations in one paragraph may usually be documented in a single note
3. The home office is separated from its ten branches: Houston Phoenix?
4. Please ship the order by November 14 or
5. All good men must

AMPERSANDS AND APOSTROPHES

Rule 1: The ampersand (&) may be used freely in tables, bills, technical material, and business names that have incorporated its use into an official, legal name. However, the ampersand should not be used in business correspondence to replace the word <u>and</u>.

> The building is located at Spring <u>and</u> Fourth streets.
> Wylie & Associates
> Century Federal Savings & Loan
> Frank's Nursery & Flower Shop

Rule 2: The apostrophe is used to form the possessive cases of nouns and certain pronouns.

A. Form the singular possessive by adding an apostrophe and s ('s) to the singular form of the noun:

> A minute's delay
> Steven's house
> everyone's time
> Ms. Adams's appointment
> The waitress's manner
> A month's work
> man's job
> sister-in-law's car

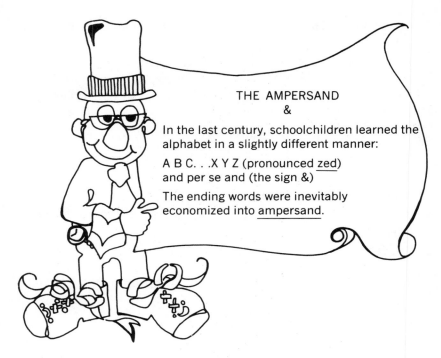

THE AMPERSAND
&

In the last century, schoolchildren learned the alphabet in a slightly different manner:

A B C. . .X Y Z (pronounced zed) and per se and (the sign &)

The ending words were inevitably economized into ampersand.

An apostrophe and s are always added to a noun ending in s or z if the s is to be pronounced as an extra syllable:

Betty's cow, Ross's move, the waitress's table. However, if the syllable is silent: Mr. Perkins' assignment, Ulysses' coat.

B. Form the plural possessive in the following way:

1. First form the plural of the noun:

   minutes
   Stevens
   Adamses
   waitresses
   months
   men
   sisters-in-law
   everyone (always singular; has no plural form)

2. If the plural form ends in s, simply add an apostrophe.

   minutes'
   Stevens'
   Adamses'
   waitresses'
   months'

3. If the plural form does not end in s, add an apostrophe and s ('s).

   men's
   sisters-in-law's

C. Special usage rules:

1. Joint ownership: John and Frank's boat
2. Separate ownership: John's and Frank's boats
3. Noun plus appositive: Mr. Garrett, the teacher's, remark
   John Fowles, the doctor's, diagnosis
4. Abbreviations: two M.D.s' opinions
   Henshey, Inc.'s, sale
5. Noun modifier exceptions: house top, counter top, television transistors, work holidays, oak table

D. The <u>genitive</u>—we may often choose between the <u>'s</u> inflection and an "of-phrase" when expressing relationship.

the purpose of the boy   = the boy's purpose
the father of the bride   = the bride's father

My Great Dane knows its master
vs.
My Great Dane knows it's master.

(Who has the upper paw?)

the meeting of the parents   = the parents' meeting
the business of Tom and Jack = Tom and Jack's business
the cars of Shirley and Jane   = Shirley's and Jane's cars

Rule 3: Personal pronouns and the relative pronoun <u>who</u> have special possessive case forms.

PRONOUN	POSSESSIVE	PRONOUN	POSSESSIVE
I	my, mine	we	our, ours
you	your, yours	they	their, theirs
she	her, hers	it	its
he	his	who	whose

Most indefinite pronouns have regular possessive forms (one's, everybody's, another's, etc.). A few of the indefinite pronouns have no regular possessive form, and an "of-phrase" is needed to indicate possession.

each, of each   all, of all
several, of several   few, of few, of a few
many, of many

PRACTICE APOSTROPHE RULES

Fill in the form of the noun or pronoun called for in each column— singular possessive, plural, and plural possessive. Leave blank forms that do not apply.

SINGULAR	SINGULAR POSSESSIVE	PLURAL	PLURAL POSSESSIVE
1. stockholder	_____	_____	_____
2. everybody*	_____	_____	_____
3. life	_____	_____	_____
4. letterhead	_____	_____	_____
5. I*	_____	_____	_____
6. brother-in-law	_____	_____	_____
7. ox	_____	_____	_____
8. party	_____	_____	_____
9. attorney general	_____	_____	_____
10. woman	_____	_____	_____
11. radio	_____	_____	_____
12. Brown & Brown*	_____	_____	_____
13. tax	_____	_____	_____
14. Adams	_____	_____	_____

	SINGULAR POSSESSIVE	PLURAL	PLURAL POSSESSIVE
15. committee	_____	_____	_____
16. county	_____	_____	_____
17. month	_____	_____	_____
18. journey	_____	_____	_____
19. anyone*	_____	_____	
20. boss	_____	_____	_____

Rule 4: An apostrophe is used to form a contraction by replacing omitted characters in words and numbers. It is always placed at the exact point of the omission.

A. Contractions:

are not	aren't
cannot	can't
could have	could've
could not	couldn't
did not	didn't
does not	doesn't
do not	don't
have not	haven't
is not	isn't
must not	mustn't
of the clock	o'clock
should have	should've
should not	shouldn't
there is, there has	there's
were not	weren't
will not	won't
would have	would've
would not	wouldn't

B. Numbers:

The class of '57 (1957)

C. Pronouns:

he'll (he will, he shall)
I'd (I had, I would)
I'll (I will, I shall)
I'm (I am)
it's (it is, it has)
I've (I have)
let's (let us)
she'd (she had, she would)
she'll (she will, she shall)
she's (she is, she has)
they'd (they did, they would)
they'll (they will, they shall)
they're (they are)
they've (they have)
we'd (we had, we would)
we'll (we will, we shall)
we're (we are)
who's (who is)
you'd (you had, you would)
you'll (you will, you shall)
you're (you are)
you've (you have)

D. Measurements:

14 feet, 9 inches: 14' 9"
10 minutes, 22 seconds: 10' 22"

Rule 5: Use an apostrophe to form the plural in certain constructions.

A. Symbols:

#'s   @'s   *'s

Eliminate the *'s from the text, please.

B. Numbers:

2's   27's   100's

Write out all 2's in the final draft.

C. Letters:

l's   m's   s's

There are too many s's in Mississippi.

D. Abbreviations:

M.D.'s   SOS's   YMCA's

There are over fifty M.D.'s in this building alone.

(Apostrophes and/or periods may be omitted when there is little chance of misreading: 1960s, YMCAs, Ks, etc.)

PRACTICE APOSTROPHE RULES

Form the plural of the following:

1. Ph.D._____
2. etc._____
3. 5_____
4. 1800_____
5. s_____
6. 100_____
7. Terry_____
8. M.D._____
9. 1960_____
10. SOS_____

11. CIA_____
12. *_____
13. t_____
14. C.O.D._____
15. Susan_____
16. Ellen_____
17. 27_____
18. IOU_____
19. L_____
20. no_____

Form the contraction of the following:

1. of the clock_____
2. would not_____
3. should not_____
4. they are_____
5. we will_____

6. you would_____
7. I am_____
8. it has_____
9. I have_____
10. it is_____

11. who is_____
12. there has_____
13. does not_____
14. cannot_____
15. she shall_____

16. I will_____
17. you had_____
18. she has_____
19. he will_____
20. I had_____

NUMBERS

There is a problem in discussing numbers. The language has several terms that are used interchangeably to refer to similar, yet distinct properties. The writing of numbers, however, is a typographical skill; i.e., the written number is visible on the page. Neither the speaker nor the listener care if the number looks like 5 or five. It is the writer who suggests importance or lack of importance by the chosen mode of expression. For the purposes of this discussion, Arabic figures will mean any representation such as 4, 9723, etc.; and spelled-out numbers or words will then be more easily identifiable.

Written Numbers

Rule 1: Numbers expressed as words are somewhat formal and tend to de-emphasize the figure.

A. Spell out isolated numbers from <u>one</u> to <u>ten</u>.

There are <u>two</u> editors and <u>five</u> assistant editors on staff.
The meeting will begin promptly at <u>nine</u> o'clock.

B. Spell out indefinite numbers expressed in one or two words.

Approximately <u>thirty</u> applicants have already been interviewed.
The conference room will hold about <u>fifteen</u> people.

C. Do not begin a sentence with an Arabic figure.

Wrong: 423 new titles were published this year.
Preferred: This year 423 new titles were published.
Wrong: 5 secretaries complete our office staff.
Preferred: Five secretaries complete our office staff.

D. Spell out fractions that are used alone as either nouns or adjectives.

Two thirds of the group should be present.
(The fraction is a noun.)

A two-thirds majority is needed.
(The fraction is a compound adjective and is therefore hyphenated.)

E. Present amounts of money in both words and Arabic figures in legal documents and very formal business letters.

Two hundred thirty-two dollars ($232)
Five thousand four hundred and fifty dollars ($5,450)

F. Except when used in days of the month or street names above tenth, spell out ordinal numbers (those expressing order or succession).

This is the Sellers Company's fifteenth year in business.
John is now living at 247 First Street in Hermosa Beach.

G. Spell out million or billion in isolated round Arabic figures to make reading easier.

$14.5 million   37 billion
 47 million   42.7 billion

H. Write out the shorter of two consecutive numbers if no punctuation mark intervenes.
(Shorter here means word length, not lesser amount.)

There are 32 twelve-page summaries on your desk.
He has eighty 79-cent lighters in his desk drawer.

PRACTICE NUMBERS RULE 1

Circle the errors in the following sentences and write the correct expression in the space provided. Write C if there is no error.

1. The 4 magazines were mailed to you on July 6.   1. _____

2. Write to the manufacturer at 1286 Twenty-third Street, Reston, VA 22090   2. _____

3. 6 leading production engineers visited the plant last Thursday.   3. _____

4. The American Patent Office receives well over 1,000,000 new patent applications a year.   4. _____

5. Advertising accounts for over 1/4 of the nonmanufacturing cost.   5. _____

6. We have 6 project managers; of the 6, 5 are college graduates.   6. _____

7. The new training class is 3/4 full.   7. _____

8. We have prepared thirty thousand 2-page brochures advertising our new product.   8. _____

9. This is the 10th annual convention.   9. _____

10. John was granted a 2-month leave of absence.   10. _____

11. We're expecting about 50 people at the conference.   11. _____

40

12. Did you know that 5 of our copyrights have already expired.   12. _____

13. The seminar begins tomorrow morning at 8 o'clock   13. _____

14. We need 42 12-inch rulers to finish the project.   14. _____

15. Mr. Jones, our president, has made Aerospace 1 of the most influential companies in the South Bay area.   15. _____

Rule 2: Numbers expressed as Arabic figures usually emphasize the figure.

A. Use Arabic figures to express most exact numbers above ten.

There are 64 daily newspapers in this state.

The new Bic pen can be purchased for 49 cents.

This report contains 47 suggestions for improving our market outlook.

We need $72 to pay for the C.O.D. (For isolated figures expressing an even dollar amount, do not use the decimal point and two zeros.)

However:

We have advertised the pens for $1.52, the yellow pads for $2.00, and the pencils for $.72 in this morning's newspaper. (Be uniform in expressing money amounts.)

Normally, amounts less than a dollar are expressed as 52 cents or 12 cents. (The cent sign (¢) is not being used.)

B. Fractions that are presented as mixed numbers (a whole Arabic figure plus the fraction) are always in figures.

3 1/2   4 1/4   19 5/6

C. Use Arabic figures to express the time of day when followed by A.M. or P.M.

The seminar lasted from 9 A.M. to 3 P.M.

If one figure has an expression of minutes, the second figure must be expressed uniformly.

The seminar lasted from 9:30 A.M. to 3:00 P.M.

D. Use commas in whole count numbers (Arabic figures) of four or more digits.

4,572   35,201

Except when the figures are used as identification numbers:

Invoice No. 5892
Order No. 72537

or when the number is a decimal:

2,142.36759

Half past the hour
of seven
in the evening

vs.

7:30 P.M.

E. Use Arabic figures to express shorter identification numbers:

Highway 5

Channel 9

Take the 405 to San Diego

F. Percentages are presented in Arabic figures with the word <u>percent</u> spelled out.

Frances is offering a 20 percent discount to Telephone Company employees.

G. When two numbers occur together and both are words or both are figures, separate them with commas.

Of the original six, five are still employed here.

Of the original 100, 42 are still employed here.

Use Arabic figures to represent exact measurements, dimensions, sizes, or temperatures.

5 pounds, 2 ounces
5 lbs. 2 oz.

68 degrees Fahrenheit
68°F

10 inches by 14 inches
10″ × 14″

H. Be uniform in expression.

The telephone company just hired 1̲4̲ engineers, 2̲4̲ computer programmers, and 6̲ secretaries.

But:

F̲i̲v̲e̲ employees worked 1̲2̲ hours of overtime this week. (Two different rules are applied to two different concepts, and the rule of uniformity does not come into play.)

PRACTICE NUMBERS RULE 2

Underline the errors in the use of numbers in the following sentences and write the correct expression in the space provided. Write C̲ if the sentence is correct.

1. We have twenty-four male and female engineers on our staff at present.   1. _____

2. Our magazine first appeared on the racks in nineteen sixty-four.   2. _____

3. His plane is due to arrive at LAX at five P.M.   3. _____

4. In 1980 13 of our original employees retired.   4. _____

5. We are manufacturing one thousand two hundred rockets an hour at this point.   5. _____

6. We are presently editing five technical manuals, 42 company handouts, and 17 brochures.   6. _____

7. The sales tax on this item amounts to one dollar and thirty-two cents.   7. _____

8. There were 72 engineers who attended the conference. Of the 72 59 attended the banquet Friday night.   8. _____

9. There are only 3 500-page reports left to do.   9. _____

10. The Company Store usually gives twenty percent discounts on items purchased.   10. _____

11. The stock closed at seven and a half.   11. _____

12. The president of our company lives just around the corner at 1993 Seventy-first Street.   12. _____

13. Our accountant appeared on the news on Channel Five last night.   13. _____

14. The temperature registered forty-two degrees Fahrenheit in mid-May.   14. _____

15. The S. L. Strong Co. paid over $5,000,000 for its new building.   15. _____

CAPITALS

A capital is formed by using an upper-case letter as the first letter of a word. We capitalize to indicate position and to create a proper noun out of a common one.

Rule 1: To indicate position, capitalize the first word in the following:

A. A sentence.

> The committee meets today.
> Today the committee meets.

B. Expressions used as a sentence (usually as an answer to a preceding question).

> Sure.   Right away.   Yes, of course.

C. An itemized list or outline.

> We need the following items:
> 1. Bond paper
> 2. Paper clips
> 3. Envelopes
> 4. Scotch tape

D. Each line of a poem.

> *I sit beside my lonely fire*
> *   And pray for wisdom yet:*
> *For calmness to remember*
> *   Or courage to forget*
> —Charles Hamilton Aïdé

E. A directly quoted sentence.

> John said, "My last day is today."

F. An independent statement following a colon.

> The advertising department agreed on one issue: The public wants higher-quality products.

G. The first word plus all principal words of a title of an article, a publication, a handbook, or a book.

> Contemporary Business Writing by Michael E. Adelstein.
> Standard and Poor's Register of Corporations, Directors on Executives
> The Dictionary of Occupational Titles (DOT)

Rule 2: The English personal pronoun I is the only personal pronoun reference consistently capitalized.

> If I were you, I'd look for a new job.

English is the only Indo-European language that capitalizes
its personal pronoun reference. Early printers capitalized
the I to avoid ambiguity between such variant
print forms as i, j, and I.

Rule 3: A <u>common noun</u> indicates a general class of people, places, objects, or qualities; while a <u>proper noun</u>, which always begins with a capital letter, indicates a <u>specific</u> person, place, quality, or thing.

Capitalize all proper nouns, proper adjectives, and their abbreviations (if any).

COMMON NOUN	PROPER NOUN	PROPER ADJECTIVE	PROPER ABBREVIATION OR NICKNAME
city	Chicago	Chicagoan	The Windy City
street	Elm Street		Elm St.
country	France	French	
day	Wednesday		Wed.
economist	Keynes	Keynesian	
man	Abraham Lincoln	Lincolnian	Honest Abe
community college	El Camino Community College		ECCC
stock exchange	The New York Stock Exchange		The Big Board
month	January		Jan.
company	General Motors		GM
man	Thomas Hubert Brown		T. H. Brown (Tom)
holiday	Thanksgiving		
state	Kansas		Sunflower State
language	Chinese	Chinese	
war	World War II		W. W. II
church	Church of England	Anglican	

Some words have lost their individualization.

    french fries   kleenex
    china dishes   pasteurize
    xerox copy

Capitalize the names of companies (but not their products), associations, independent committees and boards, political parties, and high government offices.

Ford automobile	Manhattan Beach City Council
Xerox Corporation	the Supreme Court
Federal Bureau of Investigation	Irish Spring soap
the Republican Party	Vaseline

Capitalize compass directions, seasons, celestial bodies, or names of relatives, as well as nouns followed by numbers under special circumstances.

    the Woolworth Building
    the Telephone and Xerox buildings
    Lot 15, Tract 5702
    Volume 3, Chapter 9, page 272

Highway 405 (follow the highway north)
Shorthand 207 (study shorthand)
Uncle Ralph (my uncle Ralph)
Old Man Winter (season personified)
(the winter flu season)
Southern California (a specific geographic location)
the Near East (traveling east)
King Harbor (The boat in the harbor)
the Civil War (extended war)
the Big Dipper (stars in the sky)
the Mississippi River (the Ohio and Missouri rivers)

PRACTICE CAPITALS RULES

Underline any mistakes (a word that is improperly capitalized as well as a word that needs a capital letter) in the following sentences. In the space provided, indicate the number of corrections made.

1. please meet tom at the corner of marine drive and elm street tuesday at noon.   1. _____

2. After Lunch margie inquired, "do you want me to file the Correspondence, or should i wait?"   2. _____

3. During the next Stockholders' meeting, president Chambers will introduce the new Vice-President.   3. _____

4. on saturday we had french toast, and on sunday we had omelettes.   4. _____

5. Although he had lived in the east for many years, last winter he finally returned to miami.   5. _____

6. The Company's labor day Picnic will be held a week from saturday at disneyland.   6. _____

7. Mr. john Smith of the department of the interior will deliver an address next tuesday entitled, "appreciating the national park system."   7. _____

8. The smithsonian institute, located in washington, d.c., is closed once a year, on christmas day.   8. _____

9. In desperation mary retorted, "i am a Twenty-four-year-old catholic caucasian of irish descent, and i speak both spanish and french fluently. Would you like my Social Security number also."   9. _____

47

10. Here is Kathy Holman's Address: 2472 Maryland pkw., battle creek, Michigan 59106.   10. _____

11. The Manager's flight is booked on western airlines flight 402 leaving at 8:15 A.M. on monday.   11. _____

12. the social security administration is responsible for sending my Mother her Monthly retirement check.   12. _____

13. Now that you've met Mother, i would like You to meet my Cousin Barbara.   13. _____

14. In the spring, it's hard for a student to concentrate on English and history.   14. _____

15. The vice-president of the College, William J. Watson, ph.d., introduced president Jocelyn Simon to the Student Body.   15. _____

TERMINAL PUNCTUATION

There are three separate marks used to end or terminate a sentence.

The Period

Rule 1: Use a period after an independent statement, a command, a polite request, or an indirect question.

A. An independent statement:

We provide both casualty and security protection.
This homeowner's policy provides complete coverage.
Yes. It does. (Such fragments are generally punctuated as an independent statement when they serve as answers to questions.)

B. A command:

Check every competing firm and compare prices.
Please stand up.   Open the door.

C. A polite request:

May I have a copy of last month's invoice. (No verbal response is necessary.)

D. An indirect question:

Tom asked if he might reserve the middle of June for his vacation.

Rule 2: Use periods in writing abbreviations (sometimes!).

We always call him Prof. Holt, not Mr. Holt.
Maurice Bennett is our CPA.

(Do not space after each period when typing abbreviations in capital letters, except between the two initials of a personal name: R. C. Smith. If someone uses three initials, no extra space is used: D.G.B. Jones. No periods are used when someone has become well known by his initials only: FDR, JFK, LBJ. Never end a sentence with two periods.)

Mrs. Jones is at Dr. Smith's office.

The Federal Government has established 55 mph as the standard highway speed.

W. A. Walsh and K. A. Herring have decided to join the AFL-CIO.

Some common abbreviations and acronyms should be written without periods if they are well recognized by the public. Here are a few of the most common ones.*

AAA	COBOL	IOU	TV
ABA	CIA	NAACP	TVA
ABC	CPA	NAM	TWX
AFL-CIO	FBI	NASA	UFO
AMA	FCC	NBC	VIP
AWOL	FDIC	NE	YMCA
BBC	FORTRAN	NW	WP
CAP	GNP	RFD	WPM
CBS	IBM	RN	ZIP

Rule 3: Use the period as a decimal point.

The heavy rains caused a 13.2 percent reduction in the work force.

$7.32   .331   1.7 sq. ft.

Rule 4: Use a period after a letter or number that introduces listed items (either formally or informally).

A. Formal Outline.

  I. Manuscripts
     a. Typed
       1. Pica
       2. Elite
     b. Printed
  II. Books

B. Informal listing.

The publisher is soliciting the following previously unpublished works:

1. Novels
2. Textbooks
3. Poetry

(The first word of each item is capitalized, but the period comes after the number or letter only.)

*These abbreviations are explained at the end of the book under Abbreviations and Acronyms, Section 4.

There is one conclusion that is left unconcluded—after one's signature at the end of a letter, one omits the period.

PRACTICE PERIOD RULES

Use periods where necessary in the following sentences.

1. Ask for Mr Strong
2. The new letterhead stationery has been approved
3. A common computer language used in business is called COBOL
4. The clerk did not indicate that the price is now $478 a pair
5. The 55 mph speed limit is strictly enforced by the CHP*
6. The office has two CPA's: A M Butler and B Jeff Sholls
7. Our representative in Fresno is C K Bailey on S Oakland St
8. Mr Sterman has worked for Henry H Case Co, Inc, and Booth & Booth, Ltd

9. Mr F H Boreman has just been named president of the AAA* of Southern California
10. Dr T F Williams and Prof Wadsworth will address a Westinghouse Symposium next Saturday May 7
11. Choose the color you want
12. No I won't
13. Will you please sit down
14. Prof Stetson asked the students if they had registered their complaints officially
15. May I have a copy of last month's invoice

The Question Mark

Rule 1: Use a question mark to indicate a direct question.

A. Simple question:
> How many branches does your office supervise?
> Is the meeting on Tuesday?

B. Statements used as questions:
> You did attend the conference?
> You are going?

C. Consecutive questions:
> Would you prefer Denver? Seattle? Portland?
> Are you leaving today? Tomorrow? Friday?

D. A question within parentheses or dashes:
> We visited Disneyland (have you been there?) on our vacation.

E. To express doubt:
> The negative (?) wire should be grounded.
> She was wearing an Evan Picone (?) suit.

The Exclamation Point

Rule 1: Use an exclamation point with a word or a sentence that expresses strong emotion.

> "Stop!" shouted the inspector.
> What a beautiful day!
> Gosh! I can hardly believe my promotion!

PRACTICE QUESTION MARK
AND EXCLAMATION POINT RULES

Punctuate the following sentences.

1. Look There's your flight taking off right now
2. Will you pay the bill this week or next
3. You did take messages while I was away from my desk
4. Wait
5. I can't believe it
6. Bill Stroop (have you met him) visited the branch offices last week
7. Where were you in 1962 1972 1982
8. Tom was wearing his new Botany 100 ? suit
9. Although you're busy, will you be able to get the report out by noon
10. May I hear from you by return mail
11. Wonderful
12. He asked me if I would be at the meeting
13. Should we hold the meeting on Tuesday Wednesday Thursday
14. Do you intend to change jobs
15. What a beautiful day

Grammar

Grammar is a body of generalizations about how people say things, especially how they communicate. In order to make such generalizations, we have to first agree on the terms and their meanings. The terms are usually well known, but it might be helpful to review the eight parts of speech and begin to notice how each part of speech has distinguishing characteristics that help us to understand how the English language works in business.

Eight Parts of Speech: Nouns, pronouns, verbs, adjectives, adverbs, prepositions, conjunctions, and interjections.

Although the verb is the most important part of speech in English, any discussion of the parts of speech always begins with the noun and pronoun.

NOUN

A noun is the name of a person (Kathy, woman, judge), place (Los Angeles, city, Southern California), thing (chair, phone, Bible), or abstract quality (truth, sincerity, Beauty). However, there are additional ways of identifying nouns.

A. A regular noun forms its plural by adding <u>s</u> or <u>es</u> (the only active plural ending in the language):

girl/girls   car/cars
tree/trees   watch/watches

B. A noun can be modified by certain types of words:

1. Articles—<u>a</u>, <u>an</u>, <u>the</u>

   <u>Plan moves slowly</u> is difficult to read without the article. Notice how much easier it reads when the noun is identified.

   <u>The</u> plan moves slowly.
   or
   Plan <u>the</u> moves slowly.

2. Pronominal adjectives—my, our, your, his, that, this, such, several, etc.

   <u>His</u> plan moves slowly.
   Plan <u>such</u> moves slowly.

3. Possessive nouns.

   <u>John's</u> plan moves slowly
   Plan <u>Pan Am's</u> moves slowly

PRONOUN

A <u>pronoun</u> is a noun substitute. It is essential to understand that a pronoun has no meaning, except in context. A pronoun in context takes the place of a preceding (or already stated) noun or indefinite pronoun. That noun or indefinite pronoun then becomes the <u>antecedent</u>.

Such pronouns must agree with their antecedent in case, number, and gender. Pronouns may also express point of view and thus establish the relationship of the writer to the text.

The language is not manufacturing any new pronouns, so it is a simple matter to identify the different pronoun usage forms.

Personal Pronouns: Typically, personal pronouns reflect case, number, person, and gender by a change in form.

Case	Nominative		Possessive		Objective	
Number	*Singular/ Plural*		*Singular/ Plural*		*Singular/ Plural*	
First Person	I	we	my mine	mine ours	me	us

Case	Nominative		Possessive		Objective	
Number	*Singular/ Plural*		*Singular/ Plural*		*Singular/ Plural*	
Second Person	you	you	your yours	your yours	you	you
Third Person Masculine Gender	he	they	his	their theirs	him	them
Feminine Gender	she	they	her hers	their theirs	her	them
Neuter Gender	it	they	its	their theirs	it	them

Compound Personal Pronouns: Compounds are formed by the addition of the suffix -self or -selves to the simple form and they are used to intensify or reflect back upon a preceding noun or pronoun. Never use the compound when the simple pronoun can be used.

PERSON	SINGULAR	PLURAL
First	myself	ourselves
Second	yourself	yourselves
Third	himself, herself, itself	themselves

Interrogative Pronouns: The forms who, which, and what may be used to introduce a question or an indirect question. When they do, they are called Interrogative Pronouns.

Relative Pronouns: The pronouns who, whom, whose, which, and that are used to relate one part of a sentence to another. In this respect the relative pronoun introduces the dependent adjective or noun clause and shows how that clause relates to the rest of the sentence. The pronoun can be either definite (i.e., introducing and relating the clause to a specific noun and thereby functioning as an adjective) or indefinite (i.e., introducing a clause that will function as a noun substitute).

Demonstrative Pronouns: The pronouns this, that, these, and those point out persons or things. This and these point to what is close, that and those point farther away.

Indefinite Pronouns: Roughly speaking, indefinite pronouns comprise all other pronouns and seem to share an interest in number and quantity.

SINGULAR INDICATORS		PLURAL INDICATORS	SINGULAR OR PLURAL INDICATORS
one	anyone	both	all
another	anything	few	any
anybody	each	plenty	enough

SINGULAR INDICATORS		PLURAL INDICATORS	SINGULAR OR PLURAL INDICATORS
either	nobody	several	more
everyone	someone	two, three, etc.	most
everything	something	(all numbers over one)	none
neither			some

VERB

A verb—the most important element in the English language—is a word or word group that expresses action, being, or state of being. Verbs, like nouns, have identifying characteristics.

A. A verb can be either regular or irregular.

1. A regular (or weak) verb is formed by adding -d or -ed to the present tense (walk, walked, walked) to form the past tense and past participle of the verb. This is the way we form new verbs and Americanize foreign verbs.

2. An irregular (or strong) verb forms its past tense and past participle in some other way (see, saw, seen).

B. A verb forms its singular in the third person by use of -s or -es and forms its plural by taking the -s or -es off.

Note: This is just the opposite of the noun that forms its plural by adding -s or -es.

The girl sings. (singular)

The girls sing. (plural)

C. A verb can be transitive or intransitive.

1. A transitive verb is a verb that takes an object and has voice. The voice can be either active (the subject does the action) or passive (the subject receives the action).

subj.   verb   dir. obj.
Mary hit the ball.   (active voice)

subj.   verb
The ball was hit by Mary.   (passive voice)

2. An intransitive verb does not take an object and can only be in the active voice. However, some intransitive verbs are linking verbs in that they connect a subject with its subject complement:

subj.
subj.   verb compl.
Mary is a girl.   (intransitive linking)

While others are simple intransitive:

subj.   verb
Mary speaks.   (intransitive)

A linking verb is a verb that links a subject to its complement. The word following the verb takes the reader back to the subject; that is, it completes the subject and is, therefore, called a subject complement.

The most common linking verb is any form of the verb to be (is, was, will be, has been). However, verbs having to do with the five senses are also considered to be linking verbs.

The food smells rotten.

The music sounds loud.

The dress looks old.

John feels bad.

The chicken tastes good.

Linking verbs can be followed by a noun, pronoun, or adjective as subject complement.

The boy is Tom.   (noun)

The boy is tall.   (adjective)

The boy is he.   (pronoun)

D. Verbals are certain verb forms that cannot stand by themselves but function as other parts of speech.

1. Participle—a verb form ending in -ing or -ed and used as a modifier:

Walking shoe   Covered patio
While walking to work, Mary fell down.

2. Gerund—a verb form ending in -ing and used as a noun:

subject   verb subj. complement
Walking is fun.

subject verb dir. object
I   enjoy boating.

3. Infinitive—a verb form that employs the infinitive form of the verb (to + _____) and can be used as a noun or a modifier.

To ride to school, John bought a bicycle.

subj.   prep. phrase   subj. compl.
To walk (to school) is fun.

ADJECTIVE

An adjective modifies, describes, limits, or restricts a noun or a pronoun. We recognize adjectives by position.

Attributive position—the adjective appears immediately before the noun being modified.

> pretty girl   dissatisfied worker
> old egg   young man

Appositive position—the adjectives come immediately after the noun and usually come in pairs that are considered to be nonrestrictive in nature.

> the girl, pretty and sweet, . . .
> the egg, old and moldy, . . .
> the worker, dissatisfied yet conscientious, . . .
> the woman, old and talkative, . . .

Predicate position—the adjective occurs after the linking verb and functions as a subject complement.

> The girl is pretty.   The woman was old.
>
> The egg smells moldy.   He is tall.
>
> The worker appears dissatisfied.   Everyone is busy.

ADVERB

An adverb modifies, describes, limits, or restricts a verb, adjective, or another adverb. Adverbs will often answer the question How? When? Where? or To What Degree? and How Much?

Adverbs that modify verbs:

> Joe recovered slowly.
> Mary did not do well on the test.
> Kathy hurriedly left for the airport.

Adverbs that modify adjectives:

> John is a very honest man.
> Sue types too slow for the job.
> Tom has an unusually small caseload.

Adverbs that modify adverbs:

> Tom played predictably well.
> Must you go so soon.
> Louise accepted the invitation somewhat hesitantly.

Adverbs also have a distinguishing characteristic in that they usually are formed by adding -ly to an adjective form.*

---

*There are a few nouns that can be made into adjectives by adding -ly (namely, kingly, lovely, womanly, etc.).

beautiful/beautifully
lawless/lawlessly
probable/probably
selfish/selfishly
handsome/handsomely
unusual/unusually

The adverb "hopefully" presents a special problem. It has two meanings. In writing it is used to mean "in a hopeful manner": "He faced the future hopefully." In speech (although strongly objected to by some) it can be used in the sense of "it is hoped": "Hopefully, John will be able to attend."

Finally, there are a few words that can be either an adjective or an adverb (hard, early, fast, near, late, straight). Their position in the sentence indicates their function.

    adj.   noun
He is a hard worker.
  verb   adv.
He works hard.

MEMO

This is the kind of rank insubordination
up with which I will not put!

When Winston Churchill was in charge of the Admiralty, a young lieutenant sent a memo noting the staff members' lax habit of ending their sentences with prepositions. When the memo reached Churchill's desk, he is reputed to have sent the above memo in reply.

PREPOSITION

A preposition is a word that takes an object and shows the relationship of that object to some other word in the sentence. Here is a list of the most frequently used prepositions in business communication:

about	behind	in	since
above	below	in front of	through
according to	beneath	in regard to	throughout
across	beside	in spite of	till
after	between	into	to
against	beyond	like	toward
along	but	near	under
among	by	of	until
around	by way of	off	up
as far as	down	on	upon
at	during	onto	up to
back of	except	on top of	with
because of	for	out of	within
before	from	over	without

A preposition and its object, which are usually referred to as a prepositional phrase, has become quite idiomatic in English. The advantage of a prepositional phrase is that it can be used to modify a number of different parts of speech.

Noun:	The man in the moon
Pronoun:	Everyone on the plane
Adjective:	Easy on the eye
Adverb:	Happily for her
Verb:	Walked down the road

CONJUNCTION

A conjunction is a connective. Its primary function is to join words or groups of words. Conjunctions are of three main types:

Coordinate Conjunction—The seven coordinate conjunctions are used to join items of equal value.

> and, but, or, for, nor, so, and yet

Words:

> Louise and Mary went for a walk. (Subjects)
>
> Walking and running are fun. (Gerunds)
>
> Tom typed the letter and mailed it. (Verbs)
>
> Look for the mail under the table or the chair. (Objects of the preposition under)
>
> He gave his money but not his time. (Direct objects)
>
> Suzanne is a mother and wife. (Subject complements)
>
> Tom mailed Jim and Joe a copy. (Indirect objects)

Phrases:

>Look for the mail <u>under the table</u> or <u>behind the chair</u>. (prepositional phrases)

>Walking to school and running five miles are my exercises. (gerund phrases)

>Stopping at the corner and looking both ways, Mary decided not to cross the street. (participial phrases)

>John chose <u>to learn a new trade</u> and <u>to grow with the industry</u> as much as possible. (infinitive phrases)

Clauses:

>Mary talks, but John merely listens.
>Mary talks, so John usually listens.

<u>Subordinate Conjunctions</u>—These conjunctions are used to join a dependent clause to an independent clause.

A. Adverbs—Words such as <u>if</u>, <u>because</u>, <u>while</u>, <u>since</u>, are used to introduce a dependent adverb clause and connect that clause to the independent clause in the sentence.

B. Pronouns—<u>Who</u>, <u>whom</u>, <u>which</u>, <u>that</u>, are used to introduce dependent adjective or noun clauses and connect those clauses to an independent clause.

<u>Correlative Conjunctions</u>—Correlatives always come in pairs and emphasize the fact that two ideas are involved.

>both . . . and   neither . . . nor
>either . . . or   not only . . . but also

The pairs of correlatives should be placed so that the sentence elements following them are parallel in form.

<u>Nouns</u>:

>both Kathy and Mary

<u>Pronouns</u>:

>neither she nor he

<u>Verbs</u>:

>not only wrote the book but also edited it

<u>Adjectives</u>:

>neither young nor beautiful

<u>Adverbs</u>:

>not fast but carefully

<u>Prepositional phrases</u>:

>both on the defensive and under pressure

61

Clauses:

> Fred moved to the East Coast, <u>either</u> because he liked to travel <u>or</u> because he wanted excitement.

INTERJECTION

An <u>interjection</u> is a word that is punctuated as a separate sentence and is used to denote strong feeling or emotion.

> Gosh! I didn't know you were here.
>
> Hurray! I won the toss.
>
> Obviously, expletives that are punctuated independently are considered to be interjections.
>
> Damn! I forgot my keys.

3

The Sentence

A sentence is a group of related words that expresses a complete thought. The understanding of sentence construction is essential to good business communication.

Sentence Parts: Subject, verb*, direct object, indirect object, or subject complement.

SUBJECT, VERB, DIRECT OBJECT

A simple method for analyzing a sentence consists of a series of questions:

1. What is the verb?
2. Who or what plus verb? (subject)
3. Subject plus verb whom or what? (direct object)

   *A verb is sometimes called a predicate.

The easiest way to demonstrate the method's effectiveness is to apply it to a sentence. The subject is underlined once; the verb, twice; and the direct object, three times.

<u>Mary</u> <u>made</u> a <u>copy</u>.

What is the verb?   made   (verb)

Who or what made?   Mary   (subject)

Mary made whom or what?   copy   (direct object)

INDIRECT OBJECT

<u>Mary</u> <u>made</u> Mr. Jones a <u>copy</u>.

What about Mr. Jones? Didn't Mary make the copy for Mr. Jones?

An indirect object is a noun or pronoun that designates the person to whom or for whom an action is done. It is the object of an implied preposition, and it is always found between a verb and its object.

<u>Mary</u> <u>made</u> (for) Mr. Jones a <u>copy</u>.

SUBJECT COMPLEMENT

Not all verbs, however, take an object. Sometimes the verb links a subject with a subject complement. Again, a series of questions will make the discovery process easier.

1. What is the verb?
2. Who or what plus verb? (subject)
3. Does the main word following the verb take the reader back to the subject? Yes. That word is said to complete the subject—subject complement.

The subject complement has a wavy line and an arrow pointing back to the subject.

<u>Kathy</u> <u>is</u> a computer programmer.

What is the verb?   is   (verb)

Who or what is?   Kathy   (subject)

Does the main word following the verb take the reader back to the subject? Yes.   programmer   (subject complement)

A subject complement can be a noun, an adjective, or a pronoun.

<u>Kathy</u> <u>is</u> a woman.   (noun)

<u>Kathy</u> <u>is</u> competent.   (adjective)

<u>Kathy</u> <u>is</u> she.   (pronoun)

TRANSITIVE VERB

A verb is said to be transitive when it takes an object.

Dave Turner gave the report to Mr. Jones.

A. A transitive verb will always be talking about at least two nouns.

1. One that performs the action

2. One that receives the action

B. A transitive verb can have either active or passive voice.

1. Active voice occurs when the noun performing the action is the subject.

Mary Shawhan typed the form.

2. Passive voice occurs when the noun receiving the action is the subject.

The report was typed by Mary Shawhan.

In the passive voice, the performer of the action is put into a prepositional phrase or left out of the sentence.

INTRANSITIVE VERB

A verb is said to be intransitive when it does not take an object.

A. Most intransitive verbs are said to be linking verbs in that they link a subject with its subject complement.

1. Most linking verbs are some form of the infinitive to be: am, is, are, was, were, will be, etc.

Deborah is a commercial artist.

2. A few additional verbs are also considered to be linking verbs, and these verbs usually concern the senses.

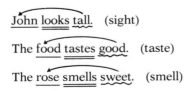

John looks tall. (sight)

The food tastes good. (taste)

The rose smells sweet. (smell)

The ability to distinguish between a complete sentence and a fragment is extremely important to the business communicator.

A fragment is an incomplete or broken thought that cannot stand alone or carry the full weight of communication.

Tom feels bad.   (kinesthetic)

The music sounds loud.   (hearing)

B.   Not all intransitive verbs have subject complements.

Kathy works.

These two words are all that is needed to express a complete thought.

Sentences can be classified according to clause structure and according to word order. It is quite important that the business communicator be able to vary sentence length and design, and understanding the choices available will aid the communicator in developing effective sentences.

CLAUSE STRUCTURE

A.   A simple sentence contains one independent clause.

David manages the farm.

The farm is managed by David.

David is a manager.

David manages well.

1. An independent clause is a group of related words that has a subject and a verb that can stand by itself.

2. A dependent clause is a group of related words that has a subject and a verb, but it *cannot* stand by itself.

B. A compound sentence contains two or more independent clauses connected in one of two ways.

1. A compound sentence can be joined by a comma and a coordinating conjunction (and, but, or, for, nor, so, or yet).

   David manages the farm, and he manages it well.

2. Without a comma and a coordinating conjunction, a compound sentence employs a semicolon to join the independent clauses.

   David manages the farm; moreover, he manages it well.

   David manages the farm; in fact, he manages it quite well.

   David manages the farm; he, however, wants to quit.

   David manages the farm; he, I believe, never will quit.

Note: the semicolon may be followed by a conjunctive adverb (moreover, therefore, however, and so on) or a transitional phrase (in fact, I believe, on the other hand, and so on) but neither is considered necessary to the connection.

C. A complex sentence contains one independent clause and one or more dependent clauses. A dependent clause may be classified in the following ways:

1. *Adjective Clause*—a dependent clause introduced by the pronoun who, whom, whose, which, or that and used to describe a noun or pronoun in the independent clause.

   The policy affects everyone who is employed.

   The policy that I just mentioned affects everyone.

   The company, which is fairly new, has recently expanded.

   The manager, whom you just met, had decided to retire.

2. *Adverb Clause*—a dependent clause introduced by an adverb such as if, because, since, while, and so on, and used to describe a verb, adjective, or adverb in the independent clause. There are two usual positions for the adverb clause in the sentence: at the end and at the beginning.

   The company will become more structured as it grows.

   As it grows, the company will become more structured.

3. *Noun Clause*—a dependent clause introduced by the pronoun who, whom, whose, which, or that and used as a noun in the sentence. A noun clause can be the subject, direct object, or object of a preposition in a complex sentence.

Who is to go has been decided. (subject)

Have you decided who is to go? (direct object)

The roses are for whoever won the race. (object of preposition)

4. *Restrictive Clause*—a clause that is necessary or essential to the meaning of the sentence; no commas are used to set off the clause.

a. Adverb clauses that appear at the end of a sentence are usually restrictive.

Mary will go if she can find a ride.

John is as interested as you are in the project.

b. Noun clauses are restrictive in nature.

That you are appreciated goes without saying.

You know that you must attend.

c. Adjective clauses can sometimes be restrictive.

The man whom you just met is the manager. (Identifies the man.)

5. *Nonrestrictive Clause*—a clause that is unnecessary or nonessential to the meaning of the sentence; commas are used to separate the clause from the rest of the sentence.

a. Adverb clauses are sometimes nonrestrictive when the information is clearly an added thought.

Mary will go, as you already know.

John is interested, as you know, in the new project.

b. Adjective clauses are mostly nonrestrictive.

Tom Smith, whom you just met, is the manager.

Note:

That always introduces a restrictive clause.

Which usually introduces a nonrestrictive clause.

Who and whom can introduce either a restrictive or a nonrestrictive clause.

D. A compound–complex sentence contains two or more independent clauses and at least one dependent clause.

John will go; Mary, whom you have never met, won't go.

If he has a ride, John will go; if he doesn't have a ride, he won't go.

WORD ORDER

There are four different labels that can be applied to a sentence in accordance with its word order: declarative, imperative, interrogative, and exclamatory.

A. A declarative sentence makes a statement that can be a fact, an opinion, or an assertion, and it can be either transitive or intransitive.

John opened the conference.   (transitive, active voice)

The conference was opened by John.   (transitive, passive voice)

John is the conference leader.   (intransitive, linking)

John is quite personable.   (intransitive, linking)

John is he.   (intransitive, linking)

John spoke for two hours.   (intransitive)

B. An imperative sentence expresses a command or a request. The subject of such a sentence is always understood to be you—the person or persons to whom the sentence is addressed.

(you)   Open the door.   (transitive)

(you)   Be here at noon.   (intransitive)

C. An interrogative sentence asks a question and is usually introduced by either a helping verb or an interrogative pronoun.

Have you seen Mr. Brown?   (transitive, active voice)

Has Mr. Brown been located?   (transitive, passive voice)

Who is the person responsible?   (intransitive, linking)

Has Mr. Brown left yet?   (intransitive)

D. An exclamatory sentence expresses strong feeling or emotion and is often introduced by what or how.

What an impression Mr. Brown made!   (transitive, active voice)

What an impression was made by Mr. Brown! (transitive, passive voice)

How easy it is!   (intransitive, linking)

Note: Some sentences are made interrogative or exclamatory by the mark of punctuation alone.

Today is the Fourth of July.
Today is the Fourth of July?
Today is the Fourth of July!

You are going.
You are going?
You are going!

Abbreviations & Acronyms

AAA American Automobile Association
AACSB American Assembly of Collegiate
Schools of Business
AAU Amateur Athletic Union
ABA American Bankers Association;
American Bar Association
abbr abbreviation
ABC American Broadcasting Company
ABCA American Business Communication
Association
AC, a.c. area code; alternating current
acct. account
acctg. accounting
A.D. Anno Domini (in the year of our Lord);
active duty; assembly district
ad hoc for this particular purpose
ADP automatic data processing
ad val <u>ad valorem</u> (in proportion to the
value)
advt. advertisement
AFL–CIO American Federation of
Labor–Congress of Industrial Organizations
AGC automatic gain control
AGR annual growth rate
agt. agent
ALA American Library Association
ALC automatic level control
AM airmail, amplitude modulation (radio)
A.M. <u>ante meridiem</u> (before noon)

AMA American Medical Association;
American Management Association
AMS Administrative Management Society
amt. amount
anon. anonymous
ans. answer
AP Associated Press
approx. approximately
APS Alphanumeric Photocomposer System
apt. apartment
ASCII American Standard Code for
Information Interchange
ASK American Simplified Keyboard
assn.; assoc. association; associate
asst. assistant
attn., Att. attention
atty. attorney
av audiovisual
ave. avenue
av., avg. average
AVT Audio Visual Tutorial (Trademark of
Media System Corporation)
AWOL absent without official leave
B.A. Bachelor of Arts
bal. balance
BBC British Broadcasting Corporation
B.C. before Christ
BCD binary-coded decimal
B/E bill of exchange

71

AGR? ? ?

Abbreviations and Acronyms
should be used with care,
lest they confuse the reader.

BF brought forward
B/L bill of lading
bldg. building
blvd. boulevard
BO buyer's option
bro., bros. brother, brothers
BS bill of sale, balance sheet
B.S. Bachelor of Science
Btu British thermal unit
cc., cc carbon copy
cc. cubic centimeter
CD certificate of deposit
CE chemical engineer; civil engineer
cen., cent. central
c f carried forward
c.f.i., CFI cost, freight, and insurance
cfm cubic feet per minute
chap., ch. chapter
chg. charge
C.H.P. California Highway Patrol

CIA Central Intelligence Agency
cm centimeter
cml. commercial
c/o care of
COBOL common business oriented language
COD cash on delivery
corp. corporation
CPA, cpa Certified Public Accountant
C.P.S. Certified Public Secretary
CPU Central Processor Unit
cr. credit; creditor
CRT cathode-ray tube
CST Central Standard Time
cu. cubic
cust. customer
CWO cash with order
D.C., DC District of Columbia
d.c. direct current
D/D demand draft

D.D. Doctor of Divinity
D.D.S. Doctor of Dental Surgery
dely. delivery
DEO department of executive officer
dep. deputy; depot
dept. department
dft. draft
dia., diam. diameter
dis. discharge; discount
disc. discount
dist. distance; distant; distribute; district
div. dividend; division
DL demand loan
dld. delivered
doz. dozen(s)
DP data processing
DPW Department of Public Works
Dr. doctor
dr. debit; debtor; dram
DSK Dvorak Simplified Keyboard
DST Daylight Savings Time
E East
ea. each
ed. edited; edition; editor; education
Ed.D. Doctor of Education
EDP electronic data process
eds. editions; editors
EDST Eastern Daylight Savings Time
e.g. exempli gratia (for example)
enc.; encl. enclosure; enclosed
Eng. engineer
Engl. English
EOF end of file
EOM end of month
Esq. Esquire
est. estimated; estate; established
EST Eastern Standard Time
et al. et alii (and others)
etc. et cetera (and so forth)
et seq. et sequentia (and those that follow)
exc. except; excellent
exch. exchange
expy. expressway
ext. extension; extended
F Fahrenheit
FB freight bill
FBI Federal Bureau of Investigation
FCC Federal Communications Commission
fed. federal; federation
ff. folios; following
FIFO first in, first out (accounting)
fig(s). figure(s)
fl. oz. fluid ounce
FM frequency modulation (radio); front matter
f.o.b., FOB free on board
FORTRAN formula translation (programming language)
frt. freight
frwy. freeway
ft. foot, feet
fwd. forward
FX foreign exchange
FYI for your information
G; g gauge; gram(s)
gal. gallon
GCT Greenwich Civil Time
gm. gram, grams
GMT Greenwich Mean Time

GNP Gross National Product
gov. governor
govt. government
gr. grain; gross; gram; grade
gr. wt. gross weight
GTC good till canceled
HF high frequency
HMS His or Her Majesty's Ship or Service
hon. honorable
hp. horsepower
hr. hour
H.R. House of Representatives (used with number for legislature bill)
hwy. highway
I.B.A. Investment Bankers Association
ibid. ibidem (in the same place)
IBM International Business Machines
ID identification date
id. idem (the same)
IDP integrated data processing
i.e. id est (that is)
IFB invitation for bids
ill. illustrated; illustration; illustrator
in. inch
Inc. incorporated
incl. including; inclusive
INS International News Service
ins. insurance
inst. institution; institute (use if part of official name)
I/O input/output device
IOU I owe you
IPN Information Processing Network
ips inches per second
IQ intelligence quotient
ital. italic; italicized
IWPA International Word Processing Association
J.P. Justice of the Peace
Jr. junior (follows name)
K Kelvin
kc kilocycle
kt. karat; kiloton
kw. kilowatt
kwh kilowatt hour
l liter; line
ll lines
lat. latitude
lb(s). pound(s)
LC letter of credit
LCL less-than-carload lot
LIFO last in, first out (accounting)
loc. cit. loco citato (in the place cited)
long. longitude
lph lines per hour (typing)
L.S. locus sigilli (place of seal)
LSI large-scale integration
Ltd. Limited (use if part of official name)
M mille (L, thousand)
m meter(s)
M.A. Master of Arts
MBS Mutual Broadcasting System
MC Master (Mistress) of Ceremonies; Member of Congress; magnetic card
M.D. Medical Doctor; Medical Department
mdse. merchandise
memo memorandum
Messrs. Messieurs (plural of Mr.)
mfg. manufacturing

mfg.   manufacture; manufacturer
mgr.   manager; monsignor
mi.   mile(s)
MICR   magnetic ink character recognition
min.   minute(s)
misc.   miscellaneous
mkt.   market
Mlle.   mademoiselle
Mme.   madame
mo.   month
mpg   miles per gallon
Mr.   Mister (abbreviation of French maister); master
Mrs.   Mistress (used as a title before the name of a married woman)
Ms.   Miss or Mrs.
MS(S)   manuscript(s)
M.S.   Master of Science
MSR   marketing service representative
mt.   mountain
MTM   Methods Time Measurement
MT/ST   Magnetic Tape/Selectric Typewriter
N   North
n/30   net in 30 days
NAACP   National Association for the Advancement of Colored People
NAM   National Association of Manufacturers
NASA   National Aeronautics and Space Administration
nat., natl.   national
N.B.   nota bene (mark well)
NBC   National Broadcasting Company
n.d.   no date
NE   Northeast
NMA   National Micrographic Association
no(s).   number(s)
NS   New Style
nt. wt.   net weight
NW   Northwest
obs.   obsolete; observation
OCP   optical character printing
OCR   optical character recognition
OK   okay
op. cit.   opere citato (in the work cited)
orig.   origin; original; originally
OS   Old Style
o/s   out of stock
oz.   ounce
p(p).   page(s)
PA   press agent; public address; power of attorney; purchasing agent
pat.   patent, patented
payt.   payment
PBS   private branch exchange; Public Broadcasting System
pd.   paid
PERT   program evaluation and review technique
pfd.   preferred
Ph.D.   Doctor of Philosophy
pk.   peck
pkg(s).   package(s)
pkwy.   parkway
pl.   plate; plural
P.M.   post meridiem (being after noon)
PO   post office; postal order; purchase order
PP   parcel post; postpaid
pr(s).   pair(s)

prem.   premium
pres.   president
prof.   professor
pro tem   pro tempore (temporarily)
P.S.   postscript
PST   Pacific Standard Time
pt.   pint; part
PTA   Parent–Teacher Association
q.   question
Q.E.D.   quod erat demonstrandum (which was to be demonstrated)
qr.   quarter; quire
qt.   quart; quantity
qts.   quarts
quot.   quotation
rd.   road
recd., rec'd.   received
ref.   referee; reference; refereed
RFD   Rural Free Delivery
RN   registered nurse
R.S.V.P.   répondez s'il vous plait (respond if you please, please reply)
rte.   route
rts.   rights (stock market)
S   South; Senate (used with number for legislative bill); series; saint
/S/   signed (before a copied signature
SA   South America; South Africa; Salvation Army
SD   sight draft; special delivery
SD-BL   sight draft, bill of lading attached
SE   Southeast; service engineer
sec.   second; section
sec., secy.   secretary
Sen.   Senator; Senate; senior
S.J.   Society of Jesus
SNOBOL   String Oriented Symbolic Language (computer language)
SO   seller's option
soc.   society
sq. ft.   square foot/feet
Sr.   senior (use after name); Señor (Spanish for Mr.)
Sra.   Señora (Spanish for Mrs.)
SRO   standing room only
Srta.   Señorita (Spanish for Miss)
SS   steamship
SSA   Social Security Administration
St.   saint
st.   street
stk.   stock
Stk. Ex.   Stock Exchange
subj.   subject
supt.   superintendent
SW   Southwest
TB   tuberculosis
t.b.   trial balance
tblsp.   tablespoon
temp.   temperature
tpke.   turnpike
treas.   treasurer; treasury
tsp.   teaspoon
TV   television
twp(s).   township(s)
TWX   teletypewriter exchange (also called telex)
U   University
u   upper; unit
uc   uppercase

UFO	unidentified flying object	**v.s.**	vide supre (see above)
UL	Underwriters' Laboratory	**VSC**	variable speed control
UN	United Nations	**VSO**	very superior old (brandy)
univ.	university; universal	**vv.**	verses
UPI	United Press International	**v.v.**	vice versa (conversely)
UPS	United Parcel Service	**W**	West
U. S.	United States	**whf.**	wharf
U.S.A., USA	United States of America	**whsle.**	wholesale
U.S.M.	United States mail	**w.i.**	when issued
U.S.M.C.	United States Marine Corps	**wk.**	week
USO	United Service Organizations	**wkly.**	weekly
V	victory; volt	**WP**	word processing
v	vector; velocity	**wpm**	words per minute
v.	vide (see)	**wt.**	weight
VHF	very high frequency	**yd.**	yard
VIP	very important person	**YM(W)CA**	Young Men's (Women's)
viz.	videlicet (namely)		Christian Association
vol(s).	volume(s)	**YM(W)HA**	Young Men's (Women's)
VOR	voice-operated relay		Hebrew Association
V.P.	vice-president	**yr.**	year
vs.	versus (against)	**ZIP**	Zone Improvement Plan
V.S.	Veterinary Surgeon		

STANDARD TWO-LETTER ZIP CODE ABBREVIATIONS OF STATES, TERRITORIES, AND POSSESSIONS OF THE UNITED STATES

Alabama	AL	Louisiana	LA
Alaska	AK	Maine	ME
American Samoa	AS	Maryland	MD
Arizona	AZ	Massachusetts	MA
Arkansas	AR	Michigan	MI
California	CA	Minnesota	MN
Canal Zone	CZ	Mississippi	MS
Colorado	CO	Missouri	MO
Connecticut	CT	Montana	MT
Delaware	DE	Nebraska	NE
District of Columbia	DC	Nevada	NV
Florida	FL	New Hampshire	NH
Georgia	GA	New Jersey	NJ
Guam	GU	New Mexico	NM
Hawaii	HI	New York	NY
Idaho	ID	North Carolina	NC
Illinois	IL	North Dakota	ND
Indiana	IN	Ohio	OH
Iowa	IA	Oklahoma	OK
Kansas	KS	Oregon	OR
Kentucky	KY	Pennsylvania	PA

Puerto Rico	PR	Vermont	VT
Rhode Island	RI	Virginia	VA
South Carolina	SC	Virgin Islands	VI
South Dakota	SD	Washington	WA
Tennessee	TN	West Virginia	WV
Texas	TX	Wisconsin	WI
Utah	UT	Wyoming	WY

TWO-LETTER ABBREVIATIONS FOR CANADIAN PROVINCES

Alberta	AB	Nova Scotia	NS
British Columbia	BC	Ontario	ON
Labrador	LB	Prince Edward Island	PE
Manitoba	MB	Quebec	PQ
New Brunswick	NB	Saskatchewan	SK
Newfoundland	NF	Yukon Territory	YT
Northwest Territories	NT		

5

Additional Exercises

REVIEW EXERCISE #1

Part A   Score _____

In the following sentences, punctuate the nonrestrictive adjective or adverb clause. Identify the adjective (adj.) or adverb (adv.) clause in the appropriate space.

1. The situation since you asked has always been the same.

   1. _____

2. The manager whom you just met is my immediate superior.

   2. _____

3. George who loves a good laugh decided not to press the issue.

   3. _____

4. Tricia Whitoff whom we have decided to support in the next election is a Democratic candidate.

   4. _____

5. The samples were in the mail as you requested
by last Tuesday.   5. _____

(10 points)

Part B

Punctuate the following sentences, and in the blank space provided
indicate whether the words:
    A. Interrupt the flow
    B. Express a parenthetical thought
    C. Are in direct address

1. You understand that as a rule we seldom make
an exception.   1. *_____

2. Ms. Ellen obviously disturbed by the news
decided to go home early.   2. _____

3. These shoes on display Mrs. Jones are our last
pair on sale.   3. _____

4. The need for an older manager on the other
hand is obvious.   4. _____

5. Mr. Jones just stood there his eyes focused
inward after he heard that the union was really
going on strike.   5. _____

6. The new manager however seemed quite
relieved by the news.   6. _____

7. Can the decision Mr. Smith be reversed?   7. _____

(14 points)

Part C

Punctuate the following sentences and indicate the reason for the
appropriate choice.
    A. An abbreviation that follows a name
    B. An "of-phrase" that follows the name of a company or a
person
    C. A nonrestrictive appositive

1. Shelly Adkins my new manager is from the
Pacific Northwest.   1. _____

2. The Sanfran Corporation of Texas has just
opened new offices in Century City.   2. _____

78

3. The company has been managed by Jerry Scott Ph.D. and Thelma Tolbert M.A. for the past three years.

3. _____

4. Our original investment a very substantial sum has shown a creditable profit.

4. _____

5. Although Steve Webber has his Ed.D. degree, he feels that he must prove himself to people like Thomas Starkly Ph.D.

5. _____

(10 points)

Part D

Punctuate the introductory elements in each sentence. Indicate in the space provided whether the element is one of the following:

   A. Adverb clause
   B. Transitional phrase
   C. Verbal phrase
   D. Nominative absolute
   E. Interjection
   F. Prepositional phrase

1. As the manager walked into the room he knew something was wrong.

1. _____

2. Gee Tom seemed upset.

2. _____

3. The story having already been told progress seemed relatively slow.

3. _____

4. On the other hand new materials were arriving daily.

4. *_____

5. To assure quality control Tom checked each order personally.

5. _____

6. Because I have been so pleased with the product I have not interviewed any other firm.

6. _____

7. In the case of severe storms the plane will be grounded.

7. _____

8. By turning around quite slowly Sue was able to catch the shoplifter in the act.

8. _____

9. In the meantime the shop has been losing money.

9. _____

10. If the case were not so self-evident I could change my opinion.

10. _____

(20 points)

Part E

Punctuate these items, and indicate in the appropriate space whether the items in a series are one of the following:
- A. Words
- B. Phrases
- C. Clauses
- D. Coordinate adjectives

1. The Sovereign Insurance Co. has district offices in Seattle Portland and Los Angeles. 1. _____

2. Jerry Toleman developed the idea Susan Sands wrote the copy and Tom Smith edited the final draft. 2. _____

3. Lucy looked in the drawer under the desk and behind the file cabinet for the missing documents. 3. _____

4. Terry Kreutzer is an assertive self-reliant young executive. 4. _____

5. The 4th 5th and 6th floors are being remodeled this month. 5. _____

6. The new manager strolled into the typing room paused by the supervisor's desk and casually asked who was in charge. 6. _____

7. The early-morning late-night schedules need to be changed. 7. _____

8. Speed and accuracy can be increased by determination practice and hard work. 8. _____

(16 Points)

Part F

Punctuate the following sentences by applying all four rules regarding the placement of commas.

1. Whether or not you agree John Russell has decided to resign his job sell his home and move to the Pacific Northwest.

2. I guess these are the last of the sale curtains Mrs. Evers.

3. To become better acquainted with Sam Johnson of Washington we need to carry on an extensive correspondence with him.

4. All things being equal my boss Dr. Blythn is usually a fair impartial judge.

5. Sally is my favorite salesperson but she needs to do something about her tendency to work work work.

6. Are you fully protected Mr. Flood against theft injury or accidental death.

7. Joyce Ulack decided to attend the banquet but she could not find a ride.

8. Linda Campbell D.D.S. has decided I believe to devote her spare time to a community reorganization project.

9. After she heard the good news Ms. Kingsley just stood there for several minutes, her eyes closed in silent prayer.

10. Picking up the pace the lead runner proceeded to set a new world's record.

11. If you had only asked Mr. Smith the outcome might have been different.*

12. H. L. Wheeler & Sons a local company has spent many hours researching that question.

13. The awards went to Richard Dowing Ph.D.; Phyllis Reynoso Ed.D.; and Bennet Wood M.D.

14. The Los Angeles Times which is a morning paper is responsible for researching and printing the morning news.

15. Do not John start work until you have developed a reasonable plan.

(30 points)

REVIEW EXERCISE #2

Part A   Score _____

Answer the following questions by writing yes or no in the space provided.

1. Expressions that begin with not, never, or seldom are set off by commas.   1. _____

2. Commas are never used for identification purposes.   2. _____

3. Questions appended to preceding statements are set off by commas.   3. _____

4. Use commas to separate items in a date.   4. _____

5. Use commas to separate items in an address when that address is written in-line.   5. _____

6. There are never special usages for comma placement. 6. _____
7. Count numbers are separated by commas. 7. _____
8. Identification numbers are separated by commas. 8. _____
9. Identical verbs in a sentence are separated by commas. 9. _____
10. Commas are used to prevent misreading. 10. _____

(10 points)

Part B

Punctuate the following and indicate the reason for your choice by writing the appropriate letter in the space provided.
A. Easily misread words
B. Identification purposes
C. Number separation
D. Clauses built on contrast

1. In the fall sale items are available. 1. _____
2. "The budget is being reviewed" responded the general manager "and a decision should be forthcoming." 2. _____
3. The longer the meeting lasted the sleepier I became. 3. _____
4. There are 4523 cartoons in this shipment alone. 4. _____
5. Mr. Garnet announced "This Friday is a holiday." 5. _____
6. The more I pressed the issue the more negative Mr. Styles became. 6. _____
7. At the hotel business was slow. 7. _____
8. Did the sales manager ask "Who made that sale " 8. _____
9. "Who made the sale " the sales manager asked. 9. _____
10. More than 1483 delegates attended the conference. 10. _____

(20 points)

82

Part C

It is also helpful to be able to recognize why commas have been used. Punctuate the following, and in the blank space choose the reason for the use of commas in each sentence.
  A. Contrasting expressions
  B. Questions appended to statements
  C. Chapter and page identification
  D. Omission of important words

1. The monthly sales meeting will be held on Wednesday not Friday.   1. _____

2. First prize for participation in this year's United Fund Campaign went to the Accounting Department; second prize to Research and Development; and third prize to Shipping.   2. _____

3. The reasons for promptness and courtesy are self-evident are they not?   3. _____

4. Mrs. Stonewell's extension is 592 not 492.   4. _____

4. Last year's budget was $1,432 wasn't it?   5. _____

6. Every page in question has already been edited hasn't it?   6. _____

7. Central Medical Group specializes in casualty insurance; Alliance in health; and Webbco in surety.   7. _____

8. By tomorrow's meeting read Chapter 7 page 42; Chapter 9 page 80; and Chapter 11 page 102.   8. _____

9. This committee was formed to reevaluate the proposal wasn't it?   9. _____

10. The supervisor's report is due on June 15 not May 15.   10. _____

(20 points)

Part D

The distinction between a restrictive and a nonrestrictive clause is very important. Punctuate the following and justify your punctuation by writing the appropriate letter in the space provided.
  A. A nonrestrictive adjective clause
  B. An adjective clause that is restrictive
  C. A nonrestrictive adverb clause
  D. An adverb clause that is restrictive

1. The Richards whom you just met are not the Richards who were my next-door neighbors.   1. _____

2. My car which I really did not like was finally sold.   2. _____

3. Tom Smith whom you have already met is my friend.   3. _____

4. I want to borrow your desk calculator after you are finished with it.   4. _____

5. We decided though it doesn't necessarily mean anything will be done that the office needs new furniture.   5. _____

6. We must go where the customers are.   6. _____

7. The district manager whom you have never met will be visiting the office on Friday.   7. _____

8. I will write a memo although I can't guarantee the results.   8. _____

9. The money that I spent is non-refundable.   9. _____

10. The manager's office which used to be mine is now a conference room.   10. _____

(20 points)

Part E

Punctuate the following sentences by applying all comma rules.

1. We had hoped that the Westwood Building would be completed by July but rainy weather strikes and supply shortages have delayed the grand opening.

2. Working hard he was able to meet the deadline.

3. To get to the root of the problem you must make an appointment to see Mr. Tameron not Mr. Jones.

4. "Profits " the chairman of the board repeated in a resigned voice "have never been lower."

5. The current list reflects price increases which were considered absolutely necessary.

6. The first offer on the building was $1.5 million; the second $1.9 million.

7. The real estate committee compared condominium prices in Marina Del Rey Venice and Redondo Beach before making its recommendation.

8. Make sure Mr. Jones that everyone gets a copy of this report.

9. "This XYZ Stereo" cooed the salesman "has a two-year money-back guarantee."

10. As of March 15 1982 our office is at its new location at 4423 Santa Monica Mall Santa Monica CA 90401.

11. Mr. Thompson I believe is in charge of ordering the paper pencils erasers etc. needed in the office.

12. Prosperity recession depression and recovery seem to be natural parts of a business cycle.

13. Equipment such as copiers duplicators and calculators is always ordered specially.

14. Merchants Bank an early bond success of mine has just opened its 14th branch office.

15. Our office should be fully automated by the year 1984.

(30 points)

REVIEW EXERCISE #3

Part A   Score _____

Answer the following questions by writing <u>agree</u> or <u>disagree</u> in the space provided.

1. A semicolon is used to separate independent clauses not joined by a comma and a coordinate conjunction.   1. _____

2. In some cases a semicolon can be a mark of elevation.   2. _____

3. A colon is never used to separate two main clauses.   3. _____

4. A colon is used after a formal introduction that includes or suggests words such as <u>the following</u>.   4. _____

5. A conjunctive adverb is a name used to describe a parenthetical adverb that follows the semicolon joining two independent clauses.   5. _____

6. A semicolon is used between items in a series when commas appear within the items.   6. _____

7. Identical verbs in a sentence are separated by a comma.   7. _____

8. Introductory elements are usually followed by a semicolon.

8. _____

9. Colons may be used to introduce a one-word appositive.

9. _____

10. A colon is used to separate the hours from the minutes when recording time.

10. _____

(20 points)

Part B

Punctuate the following sentences and indicate in the appropriate space whether the word(s) underlined can be termed one of the following:

    A. Conjunctive adverb
    B. Transitional expression
    C. Parenthetical expression

1. Walcott Inc. shipped the new furniture two weeks ago <u>however</u> it was delayed in transit.

1. _____

2. This building is scheduled to be demolished June 15 the new building <u>moreover</u> is not scheduled for completion until June 1985.

2. _____

3. The plant will not be ready for production by October <u>in other words</u> we will be forced to delay the start of the new project.

3. _____

4. We asked personnel to begin replacement proceedings for hiring another secretary <u>hence</u> the ad in this morning's classified advertising section.

4. _____

5. The purpose of the memo is to change the hiring policy <u>in other words</u> we want Mr. Sparyak to follow company policy more closely.

5. _____

6. The decision was not easy <u>on the other hand</u> the choice was clear.

6. _____

7. Mrs. Bentley has continuously ignored our requests <u>obviously</u> she does not intend to cooperate.

7. _____

8. The production department has been severely cut back the accounting department <u>on the other hand</u> has hired two new employees.

8. _____

9. We asked you to delay the action <u>in other words</u> we want to reconsider the project.

9. _____

10. Ms. Williams was not involved in the planning stage <u>however</u> she has been very active in production.　10. _____

11. The sandwiches seemed stale <u>otherwise</u> it was a successful brunch.　11. _____

12. Mrs. Wilson has been in advertising for the past four years <u>actually</u> her degree in Marketing has served her well in her career.　12. _____

13. The wood paneling suits this office perfectly the pink light fixture <u>on the other hand</u> seems to detract from the total effect.　13. _____

14. Ed Jones is usually fair <u>as a result</u> the people who work for him admire him greatly.　14. _____

15. The position has been filled already <u>still</u> you could submit a resume.　15. _____

Part C

Punctuate the following by applying the rule concerning the special usage of the colon.

about four in the afternoon

Dear Ms. Wilson

Gentlemen

To Whom It May Concern

7 18 A.M.

7 45 P.M.

Dear Dr. Johnson

12 midnight

2 35 P.M.

Dear Bishop Clark

(10 points)

Part D

Follow the directions to complete each sentence.

1. Write a sentence followed by one word.
2. Write a sentence that uses a colon to introduce a list.
3. Write a sentence that introduces a list and does not use words such as <u>namely</u> or <u>for example</u>.

(10 points)

Part E

Punctuate the following by applying all punctuation rules studied thus far.

1. In the morning the school is never open before 7 45 A.M. however it stays open every evening until 9 00 P.M.

2. A nurse may be trained at a hospital a university or both a doctor on the other hand is always university trained.

3. College students should I believe make an effort to learn as much as possible so they can apply their knowledge when they enter the labor force.*

4. Mr. Cross asked his assistant to telephone for a prompt reliable and trustworthy messenger.

5. By finding ways to cut down on unnecessary costs the good manager demonstrates an interest in efficiency as well as cost effectiveness.

6. An outgoing warm personality is an asset to any person in business but nothing takes the place of experience and knowledge.

7. The cleaning crew plan to wax the floor and clean the windows in the reception area next week this week they will shampoo the rugs and wash down the walls.

8. The main problem with the new design is the cost the solution however seems very near at hand.

9. We have in stock at this writing the following sizes A9613 H9472 and J9823.*

10. Your suggestion I'm sorry to say came at a time when we had no budget allowance for new furniture next year's budget should rectify that problem.

11. The Ajax Agency can always be counted on for one thing creativity.

12. Ted Bob and Alice worked late four nights this week moreover they plan to spend at least Saturday afternoon completing the layout.

13. You might say Mr. Merriweather that the success of the project depends upon you.

14. This has not been Mr. Atkins day He arrived late for the executive meeting broke his reading glasses and tripped over Mr. Crump's briefcase.

15. Yes Mr. Sandoval can meet with you today however he won't be free until after 2 30 this afternoon.

(30 points)

REVIEW EXERCISE #4

Part A   Score _____

Rewrite the following so that a compound adjective containing at least one hyphen is formed.

1. The novel is never to be forgotten.

   _____

2. This extension is only for a short term.

   _____

3. The museum specializes in paintings of the fifteenth century.

   _____

4. We cruised the harbor in a sailboat that was 16 feet long.

   _____

5. The manager looks friendly.

   _____

6. The budget estimate should be brought up to date.

   _____

7. The test should have every blank filled in.

   _____

8. There is a speed trap of 25 miles per hour close to the office.

   _____

9. The beginning salary is $10,000 a year.

   _____

10. His next business trip will last three weeks.

   _____

(20 points)

Part B

Change the punctuation in the following sentences and give the reason for the change in the appropriate space. A dash can be used:

    A.   For a nonrestrictive phrase or clause
    B.   To introduce a list
    C.   To emphasize final words

1. Mr. Foinsworth has but one choice: success!   1. _____

2. Several employees have worked for this firm for over fifteen years; for example, Kristen Kauffman, Linda Davis, and Mark Andrew.

2. _____

3. I can't overstate the present need: cost control.

3. _____

4. Our quarterly magazine, which you have contested, was recently discontinued.

4. _____

5. Our new building, despite major setbacks, is finally ready for inspection.

5. _____

6. The accounting department, as you well know, has had its ups and downs during the past year.

6. _____

7. There's one item we forgot: the word processor.

7. _____

8. The opposition by several committee members, namely Steven Blumberg, Dave Walker, and Tom Lesser, was quite vocal.

8. _____

9. Mr. Jarvis did not consider an important factor: recession.

9. _____

10. These courses are required of all computer majors; namely, physics, math, and statistics.

10. _____

11. Mr. Strong's visit will convince you, we hope, that our company can handle your casualty line.

11. _____

12. That particular section of highway, which buckled in the heat, will take nine months to repair.

12. _____

13. We can have Robert reorganize the bookshelves, if you think it's needed, so that all the customer files will be together.

13. _____

14. Most visitors to Washington have one major stop in mind: the White House.

14. _____

15. Star Williams, to prove her point, found the letter within three minutes.

15. _____

(30 points)

Part C

Insert hyphens where necessary in the following expressions.

two thirds of the country
three fourths vote
self assured

re cover the sofa
well behaved child
An ad hoc committee

self ish
fifty five
president elect
re form the voter
thirty three
my great aunt Jane
two fisted attitude

a hit or miss approach
old fashioned girl
double spaced
fire resistant material
re sign the position
much needed reforms
ex president

(20 points)

Part D

Punctuate the following sentences, applying all the rules on commas, semicolons, colons, dashes, and hyphens. Punctuate for emphasis, except when specifically directed otherwise.

1. The office needs one thing more room.*
2. Christine Duvall who is in charge of shipping is an invaluable asset to the company in other words management has no intention of replacing her.
3. Three competing agencies Jay Walker Brown & Little and Millers are submitting bids on Thursday.
4. (One regular punctuation and one emphatic punctuation.) Joyce Andrews much to everyone's surprise has become an efficient manager enviably efficient.
5. Payroll looked everywhere so it was claimed for my missing check it was finally found behind the credenza.
6. Three fourths of our employees drive more than twenty minutes each way to work unfortunately we have no ride sharing plan in effect.
7. (Punctuate in the regular way.) The following items are needed by Friday a filled in insurance form a signed W-2 form and two copies of your degree.
8. Reading your credentials I find that you are exactly the person we have been looking for can you start Monday?
9. The problem the only problem that needs solving is outlined in my report.
10. Our employees have never been accident prone.
11. Today not tomorrow is our company's twenty fifth anniversary.
12. That desk has serious problems problems that our repairman has not even considered.
13. Are you applying for a part time or full time position?

14. Experience plus intelligence that's the secret to success.

15. (Punctuate in the regular way.) This new plan must be cost effective or management will turn it down.

(30 points)

REVIEW EXERCISE #5

Part A   Score _____

Please indicate your response to the following statements by writing <u>agree</u> or <u>disagree</u> in the appropriate space.

1. A parenthetical statement that appears within the first of two clauses is punctuated as part of that clause.   1. _____

2. Never put a comma before an opening parenthesis.   2. _____

3. Parentheses are used to set off and de-emphasize.   3. _____

4. Brackets are only used within parentheses.   4. _____

5. The word <u>sic</u> means "thus," and indicates that the author is being quoted exactly.   5. _____

6. Parentheses are used to enclose numbers or letters that identify items in series that appear <u>in-line</u>.   6. _____

7. Parenthetical expressions that are complete sentences are never punctuated as such.   7. _____

8. Never put a mark of punctuation such as a question mark or an exclamation point within parentheses by itself.   8. _____

9. Dollar amounts can be written out and placed in parentheses as arabic numbers plus dollar sign.   9. _____

10. Brackets can be used to inform the reader of added emphasis.   10. _____

(20 points)

Part B

Indicate what marks of punctuation—parentheses or brackets—are ordinarily used for the purposes described.

1. To give added information at the end of a quotation.   1. _____

2. To set off a parenthetical expression appearing in an introductory clause.   2. _____

3. To set off parenthetical expressions that are complete sentences.   3. _____

4. To substitute for a parenthesis when appearing inside existing parentheses.   4. _____

5. To indicate bibliographic reference.   5. _____

6. To enclose numbers or letters that identify items in a series or list written in-line.   6. _____

7. To de-emphasize a nonrestrictive phrase.   7. _____

8. To identify a mistake in a direct quotation.   8. _____

9. To set off a single word as parenthetical.   9. _____

10. To surround the word sic.   10. _____

(20 points)

Part C

Punctuate the following sentences by applying all of the rules of punctuation learned thus far.

1. Our company manufactures radios TV sets refrigerators and microwave ovens and we are looking for ways to expand into other more diversified? fields.

2. The efficient receptionist whether a man or a woman is an undeniable asset to a company.*

3. Tact wisdom and courtesy these are marks of the progressive manager.

4. The career oriented college graduate is looking for a chance to break into a fast growing profitable respected profession.

5. We have branch offices in Detroit St. Louis Cleveland and New York at present moreover we are hoping to establish a London England branch by the end of the fiscal year.

6. A new firm Career Inc.? has just taken over the fifth floor of this building. (Uncertainty about the company name.)

7. The article stated "The losses to four brokerage house sic are currently estimated at over $4 million."

8. The markup for retailers stores banks and mail order firms would be substantial however the projection assumes a complete sellout.

9. When we visited the Akron plant we could not compare it with the home office plant.

10. Mr. Herring conducts most of his business by phone however he begins each morning by reading his mail.

11. The cufflinks are in the mail you will notice see the spring 1982 catalog that we save you a substantial amount if you send in your order within five 5 days.

12. Your business like any other new business will benefit from experience.*

13. Some departments are experiencing high turnover this department however has an excellent employee record.

14. Have your representative Mr. Burn? contact Mr. Feidler immediately.

15. The test was easy wasn't it?

(60 points)

REVIEW EXERCISE #6

Part A Score _____

Answer <u>true</u> or <u>false</u> to the following statements concerning the use of quotation marks.

1. Direct quotations are the exact words used by a writer or speaker. 1. _____

2. Titles of major literary works usually appear in italics or are underlined. 2. _____

3. Titles of movies are also in italics. 3. _____

4. Periods and commas always appear inside the closing quotation mark. 4. _____

5. Semicolons and colons always appear outside the closing quotation mark. 5. _____

6. Short expressions are never used in an unconventional manner in this language. 6. _____

7. A question mark, an exclamation mark, or a dash can appear either inside or outside a closing quotation mark. 7. _____

8. Titles of minor works usually appear in quotation marks. 8. _____

9. An indirect quotation is always set off by
quotation marks. 9. _____

10. Technical words can be emphasized or clarified
by the use of quotation marks. 10. _____

(20 points)

Part B

Use quotation marks or an underline to indicate whether the
following titles are minor or major works.

Essays in Biography (Book)
by John Maynard Keynes

The Wall Street Journal
(Newspaper)

Fortune (Magazine)

Raiders of the Lost Ark
(Movie)

Smithsonian (Magazine)

Let It Be (Song) by John Lennon

The Atlantic Monthly
(Magazine)

The Affluent Society (Book)
by John Kenneth Galbraith

The Raven (Poem)
by Edgar Allen Poe

Goodbye Columbus (Short Story)
by Phillip Roth

(20 points)

Part C

Punctuate the following by adding quotation marks or underlining
where necessary.

1. Mrs. Elliott asked Is organizational ability really important for a
mid-management position?

2. Is organizational ability asked Mrs. Elliott really important for a
mid-management position?

3. Is organizational ability really important for a mid-management position? asked Mrs. Elliott.

4. Was it Barbara McCauley who asked Is the Executive Club for
men only?

5. (Punctuate only the title Executive Club.) Was it Barbara
McCauley who asked about the location of the Executive Club?

6. Will you please make a copy of the article Over-the-Counter
Markets in today's Wall Street Journal? asked Robert Jones.

7. Roger interrupted us by saying Let me read you a quote from
James C. Sanders the new chief of the Small Business Admin-

istration Few businesses can afford to borrow at current high interest rates.

8. Was it Barbara McCauley who asked if the Executive Club was for men only?

9. Did you see the article about the Small Business Administration in The Wall Street Journal?

10. Look up the verb savage for me.

(20 points)

Part D

Punctuate the following, employing all of the rules of punctuation studied thus far. You will be advised if material has been omitted from a quotation.

1. Writers frequently spell words from memory but that spelling is often incorrect.

2. To achieve success said the general manager you must be willing to devote long difficult hours to learning your trade.

3. There are features in this agreement as it stands at present that are not satisfactory to the union replied the business agent.

4. (Something has been left out) Yes gentlemen business success is largely a matter of using what you have droned the general manager.

5. Do not accelerate the engine before it is warm cold oil does not lubricate.

6. It is a pleasure to recommend Miss Paulo to anyone who is looking for a competent obliging and efficient stenographer wrote Mr. Rogus.

7. If a court appearance is necessary these terms will not apply the fee will have to be arranged for in advance.

8. Our statements are based on exact knowledge not vague hopes.

9. Any firm offering information plus service is bound to succeed isn't it?

10. Lyle Holmes founded this company with only $1,000 and a dream see page 20 and its success came slowly

(40 points)

REVIEW EXERCISE #7

Part A

Score _____

Write the contracted form in the space provided.

1. you are _____
2. 1937 _____
3. do not _____
4. 11 feet, 2 inches _____
5. of the clock _____

6. would not _____
7. 5 minutes, 30 seconds _____
8. 1962 _____
9. have not _____
10. who is _____

(20 points)

Part B

Rewrite the following phrases in the possessive form.

1. The daughter of my boss _____
2. The notes of the typists _____
3. The statement of the vice-president _____
4. The children of my brothers-in-law _____
5. The finances of the firm _____
6. The meeting of the directors _____
7. The suits of the men _____
8. The editorial in the <u>Los Angeles Times</u> _____
9. The policy of R. W. Murphy _____
10. The report of the committee _____
11. A delay of a month _____
12. The home of Susan and George _____
13. The sale of Henchey, Inc. _____
14. The families of John and Frank _____
15. The project of four weeks _____

(30 points)

Part C

In the following sentences, indicate the correct choice by underlining the appropriate word from each group in parentheses.

1. Tell Mr. Smith (whose, who's) program is more feasible, mine or (hers, her's).

2. (Its, It's) going to be a long meeting.
3. The messengers have been here and (there, they're, their) certain the packages are (theirs, their's, theres, there's).
4. Close the letter, (yours, your's) truly.
5. This report of (his, his') is extremely clear in (its, it's) presentation of the facts.
6. A representative of (our's, ours) is arranging for (they're, their) merger.
7. Good government is (everyones, everyones', everyone's) concern and depends on (everybodys, everybodys', everybody's) cooperation and support.
8. Jack Selby, (whose, who's) assignment includes programming the computer, wants to become a systems analyst eventually.
9. The personnel department is dedicated to work on (your're, your) behalf and (my, mine).
10. (Whose, Who's) the young woman in charge of accounts payable?
11. When the new IBM Selectric will be delivered is (anybodies, anybody's) guess.
12. We have sent the branch managers (our's, ours); however, some of the managers are slow in sending us (theirs, they'res, their's).
13. We owe a vote of gratitude to (our, our's) panel of experts for (its, it's) excellent presentation.
14. All employees are eligible for a 20 percent discount on the price of (they're, their) tickets.
15. (Were, We're) the management team responsible for (this, these) project.

(30 points)

REVIEW EXERCISE #8

Part A   Score _____

Change the following cardinal Arabic numbers into the appropriate written-out ordinal numbers. (If necessary, use a dictionary.)

1.	14_____	4.	49_____
2.	77_____	5.	86_____
3.	12_____	6.	72_____

7. 21_____   **9.** 35_____

8. 43_____   **10.** 27_____

(20 points)

Part B

Indicate in the appropriate blanks whether you agree (A) or disagree (D) with the following statements.

1. Arabic figures can begin sentences.   1. _____

2. Expressing numbers as words tends to de-emphasize the number.   2. _____

3. Spell out isolated numbers from <u>one</u> to <u>ten</u>.   3. _____

4. Spell out all ordinal numbers.   4. _____

5. Spelling out isolated round numbers such as <u>million</u> or <u>billion</u> makes reading easier.   5. _____

6. Arabic figures are used to express most exact numbers above ten.   6. _____

7. Consistency is necessary when expressing numbers in words or Arabic figures.   7. _____

8. The time of day should always be written out in words.   8. _____

9. Identification numbers are expressed and punctuated in the same manner as count numbers.   9. _____

10. Percentages are presented in Arabic figures with the word <u>percent</u> spelled out.   10. _____

11. Write out the shorter of two consecutive numbers if no punctuation mark intervenes.   11. _____

12. When two numbers occur together and both are either words or Arabic figures, separate them with commas.   12. _____

13. Use commas in whole count numbers of four or more digits.   13. _____

14. Never spell out indefinite numbers.   14. _____

15. Arabic figure expression is used for emphasis.   15. _____

(30 points)

Part C

If no change needs to be made in the following sentences, write <u>C</u> for <u>correct</u> in the space provided. If there is an error, underscore

99

the error and write the correct written figure in the space provided. Many sentences have more than one error.

1. If I'm not there by 7 o'clock, turn the extra 4 tickets back into the box office and credit my name.

1. _____

2. The $.69 yellow pad now sells for $.98.

2. _____

3. Our new vice-president is only about 40 years old, but he has been with this company going on his 15th year.

3. *_____

4. John Smothers will be attending a seminar tomorrow from 9:00 A.M. until 2:30 P.M.

4. _____

5. The new secretary will be here at 9 o'clock on the 5 of next month.

5. *_____

6. 2,000 or more people voted in the 21 District.

6. *_____

7. The pamphlet we have been working on for over 6 weeks will not be ready for another 5 days.

7. _____

8. Where did you store the 17 69-cent envelopes and the 45 5-cent stamps that I purchased yesterday.

8. _____

9. I interviewed 14 engineers, 7 programmers, and 22 cost accountants on a recent 5-day recruiting trip.

9. _____

10. The new security guard stands six feet seven inches tall and weighs two hundred twenty-five pounds.

10. *_____

11. Many of the applicants had difficulty in adding 3 1/4, one half, and two thirds.

11. _____

12. The new Selectric typewriter weighs only 9 pounds and is fully guaranteed for 2 years.

12. _____

13. The magazine contains over one hundred suggestions for improving safety standards over a 5-state area.

13. _____

14. We have not talked to Mr. Smith since the 3 of April, and we have over fifty new orders to place with him.

14 *_____

15. The records indicate that John paid $49.72 for his hotel room, $90 for meals, and $18.75 for telephone calls.

15. _____

16. Sander J. Caldwell has made over $1,000,000 in insurance.

16. _____

17. The plane, Western Flight seventy-two, leaves for Seattle at six forty-two P.M.

17. _____

18. Our offices close promptly at 5:30 P.M. during the winter months and at 4:40 P.M. during the summer months.

18. _____

19. Even if you have as few as 5 phones, you can take advantage of the Executive electronic system.

19. _____

20. The corporate library has over 27 business management and business communications books in its five branch offices.

20. _____

21. Your check for one thousand two hundred five dollars arrived on May 21st.

21. _____

22. The board meeting lasted from one-thirty till five P.M.

22. _____

23. 1/2 of the positions in our San Diego office are filled by people with 5 years' experience.

23. _____

24. We have a scheduled meeting with five union representatives at 9:30 tomorrow morning.

24. _____

25. Whereas a product may take from six to 36 months in design, its actual success is evident within 3 months of being on the market.

25. _____

(50 points)

REVIEW EXERCISE #9

Part A   Score _____

Organize the following list of words into the proper categories.

Georgia	Doctoral	Honest Abe	English
New York	Big Apple	man	doctor
Eng.	GA	city	country
Abraham Lincoln	England	Georgian	New Yorker
state	Ph.D.	Lincolnian	Doctor of Philosophy

COMMON NOUN	PROPER NOUN	PROPER ADJECTIVE	PROPER ABBREVIATION OR NICKNAME
_____	_____	_____	_____
_____	_____	_____	_____
_____	_____	_____	_____
_____	_____	_____	_____
_____	_____	_____	_____

(40 points)

101

Part B

Underline any mistake in capitalization or punctuation in each of the following sentences and indicate the number of mistakes in the space provided.

1. the missouri and mississippi rivers flow from North to south; the ohio river flows from east to west. 1. _____

2. The Southern part of texas, where I was born, is hottest during the summer. 2. _____

3. Mrs Mitchell the department Supervisor of jacobs Department store spoke at the board of directors meeting Yesterday. 3. _____

4. The Director of the Lakeland hotel is john Golis jr., the Assistant director is still Marion Freeman. 4. _____

5. Every person of spanish descent should know that south america is represented at the united Nations. 5. _____

6. Our Attorney, Mr. anthony d. dowling, jr., assured us of our Rights against the Alliance insurance company. 6. _____

7. The Medlock tool co. appreciates the information received from the Corpus Christi board of Education on January 17. 7. _____

8. The southern California Advertising Agency of Bemis, Bormer, and Beard offers exceptional opportunities for Employment as far South as San Diego. 8. _____

9. The president left the white house by Helicopter at Noon and arrived at camp david within the Hour. 9. _____

10. The Point, a Motel/Hotel in phoenix, Arizona, offers tennis Courts, a String of fine saddle horses, and an excellent Golf Course for guests. 10. _____

11. Why don't you travel to san Francisco up Scenic highway 1 instead of going through the monterey peninsula? 11. _____

12. The Hotel where we like to stay in Carmel is of moorish design with wide spanish balconies. 12. _____

13. His Resumé indicates that his four years in High School and his two years in Community College were supported by part-time work at sears. 13. _____

102

14. As an Aid to our Dealers, we have arranged a tour at our factory on june 9 and 10.　　14. _____

15. A Savings Account, however, draws exceptional Interest Rates at santa monica bank if a deposit is made before the 15th of each Month.　　15. _____

(60 points)

REVIEW EXERCISE #10

Part A

Form the following groups of words into appropriate indented lists.

1. Martin will be responsible for the following: books, tests, and brochures.

2. The company has branch offices in the following states: Texas, Oklahoma, Arizona, and Nevada.

3. Each desk should have certain supplies: manuscript paper, typewriter ribbons, and correction fluid.

4. Will you please submit the report in the usual manner: typed, double-spaced, summarized, and indexed.

(20 points)

Part B

Vocal and facial expression transmit strong emotions to the listener. We can do the same thing with punctuation marks. Punctuate each group of words in three different ways.

Will you please go home now	You will be there
Will you please go home now	You will be there
Will you please go home now	You will be there
You know the answer	The report was a success
You know the answer	The report was a success
You know the answer	The report was a success

(20 points)

Part C

Write out the meaning of each abbreviation or acronym given.

1. AMA _____
2. CIA _____
3. FBI _____
4. IBM _____
5. NASA _____
6. RN _____
7. IOU _____
8. WP _____
9. TV _____
10. VIP _____
11. Messrs _____
12. NB _____
13. rd. _____
14. secy _____
15. approx. _____
16. BS _____
17. Corp. _____
18. dft. _____
19. expy _____
20. in. _____

Part D

Punctuate the following sentences.

1. How many policies did you sell in August in September in October

2. Did you learn FORTRAN first

3. Ouch Try to be more careful

4. (A Question) You are sure, Shirley, that you filed the papers

5. Our new building is located at the corner of Olympic Blvd and National Ave

6. The average family in L A is spending over 37 7 percent of its income on housing *

7. Will you please sign the enclosed voucher and return it to our office within the next three days

8. Is he still the No 1 salesman at Haley Inc

9. One of our underwriters (was it Martin) wrote you concerning cancellation of the bond

10. The sale offers savings ranging from $10 99 to $599 00 on floor samples
11. If he were a member of the California AAA he would enjoy the benefit of on the road repair service *
12. What a stirring rendition of the 1812 Overture
13. Have you ever used the abbreviation i e
14. H R Sellers Inc had a very good year in 1979
15. Will you please mail this letter immediately
16. More than 12 7 percent of the office staff had the flu in February
17. Has the manager approved your suggestion "All personnel changes must be in writing"
18. (An Exclamation) That was a long hike
19. He asked if J L Stevens could work overtime this weekend
20. Sure he did

6

Final Review

(Choose one of the following letters and punctuate, applying all the punctuation rules outlined in this book.)

---

march 5 1982

randall and randall inc
37 tailor avenue
englewood cliffs new jersey 07013

gentlemen

janet deserves the highest rating for both her scholarly and creative ability as a student in my class business english 207 she has contributed significantly to the improved attitude of many of her peers she has always appeared totally involved in the subject matter letter writing and she has created enthusiasm for the understanding of the communication process

i feel extremely fortunate to have known janet as both a student and i believe a friend after only a short time in the class i became aware of janet s depth of knowledge where appreciation of english is concerned this is particularly impressive since english is not her first language

janet s good humor zest and careful preparation contribute to her classroom presence and make knowing her a pleasure she upholds her end of an agreement is aware of the details that make things work and is a delightful person to meet

sincerely yours

---

january 14 1982

medical planning association
18750 wilshire blvd
santa monica california 90401

medical planning associates

i am replying to your advertisement for a librarian/researcher/rn in the june 6 1982 edition of the los angeles times

i am a registered nurse who will be graduating from a secretarial program at the end of june i am planning to make a career change however i would consider utilizing my nursing background my experience includes office industrial and hospital nursing

enclosed is a resumé that shows i do have many of the qualifications that you are seeking although i do not have any Computer skills i would be eager to learn

i would be interested in an interview to discuss how my background may relate to your needs

yours truly

---

march 15 1983

mr dennis ely
loyalty finance company
1219 blue crest drive
tampa florida 33614

dear mr ely

congratulations on your opening in tampa last week

we have the one hundred fifty pounds 150 of hammermill bond paper in stock we would be happy to print your Logo on the paper with the royal blue ink you specified if you like the royal blue ink on the hammermill bond is quite impressive you ve made an excellent choice

as we have printed on the interior of the cover page of the catalog you ordered from we have stringent credit requirements because of the volume of mail order business we do one of our requirements is that the firms to which we extend credit need to have been in business at their current address for at least one calendar year before becoming eligible.

we will be happy to complete processing your order if you care to send us cash check or money order if you prefer you can call your payment in by using any nationally recognized Credit Card

best wishes for a prosperous and successful year and please feel free to reapply next year

sincerely yours

---

december 13 1982

mr owen m peck
peck & peck inc
627 manchester ave
anaheim california 92802

dear mr peck

thank you for your letter of november 28th with enclosures

your comment that c p a prepared statements would be forthcoming was most welcome as a review of the current file information makes it apparent that our present case is a people case plus three nubian goats this is the first time i have ever bonded three nubian goats or for that matter even one nubian goat but i have admired the breed from afar for years and have always thought the prospect breathtaking

i seem to be a bit short of background detail on the Principals the jacksons that is not the goats and i would appreciate having the enclosed contractor s questionnaire filled out so that we may fill in some of the gaps

you mentioned in your letter that you had steered the jacksons to their Bank and i think that is an excellent idea i have a most entertaining mental image of them in conference with their loan officer accompanied by their 3 nubian goats

it might also be wise to discuss their life insurance program i wonder if your life insurance Associate has ever ordered a physical on a nubian goat

regards

ALTERNATE REVIEW

Part I

Place a check mark in front of the letter to indicate the correct interpretation for the comma usage.

1. Shelly Adkins, my new manager, is from the Pacific Northwest.
   A. An abbreviation that follows a name
   B. An "of phrase" that follows a name
   C. A nonrestrictive appositive

2. Gee, Tom seemed upset.
   A. An adverb clause
   B. An interjection
   C. A prepositional phrase

3. These shoes on display, Mrs. Jones, are the last pair on sale.
   A. A noun in direct address
   B. Expresses a parenthetical thought
   C. Interrupts the flow

4. In the fall, sale items are available.
   A. Clauses built on contrast
   B. Easily misread words
   C. Identification purposes

5. The monthly sales meeting will be held on Wednesday, not Friday.
   A. Contrasting expression
   B. Omission of important words
   C. Questions appended to statements

6. On the other hand, new materials are arriving daily.
   A. Adverb clause
   B. Transitional phrase
   C. Verbal phrase

7. Terry Kreutzer is an assertive, self-reliant young executive.
   A. Words in a series
   B. Clauses in a series
   C. Coordinate adjectives

8. The Sanfran Corporation, of Texas, has just opened new offices in Century City.
   A. An "of phrase" that follows a name
   B. An abbreviation that follows a name
   C. A nonrestrictive appositive

9. To assure quality control, Tom checked each order personally.
   A. Adverb clause
   B. Verbal phrase
   C. Prepositional phrase

10. Ms. Ellen, obviously disturbed by the news, decided to go home early.
    A. A noun in direct address
    B. An adverb clause
    C. Interrupts the flow

11. More than 1,483 delegates attended the conference.
    A. Easily misread words
    B. Number separation
    C. Identification purposes

12. The reasons for promptness and courtesy are self-evident, are they not?
    A. Contrasting expressions
    B. Questions appended to statements
    C. Omission of important words

13. The new manager strolled into the typing room, paused by the supervisor's desk, and casually asked who was in charge.
    A. Phrases in a series
    B. Clauses in a series
    C. Coordinate adjectives

14. Although Steve Webber has his Ed.D. degree, he feels he must prove himself constantly.
    A. Verbal phrase
    B. Prepositional phrase
    C. Adverb clause

15. The company has been managed by Jerry Scott, Ph.D., and Thelma Tolbert, M.A., for the past three years.
    A. An abbreviation that follows the name
    B. An "of-phrase" that follows the name
    C. A nonrestrictive appositive

16. The story having already been told, progress seemed relatively slow.
    A. Adverb clause
    B. Verbal phrase
    C. Nominative absolute

17. The new manager, however, seemed quite relieved by the news.
    A. Interrupts the flow
    B. Expresses a parenthetical thought
    C. Can be in direct address

18. The more I pressed the issue, the more negative Mr. Styles became.
  A. Clauses built on contrast
  B. Number separation
  C. Easily misread words

19. Mrs. Stonewell's extension is 592, not 492.
  A. Contrasting expressions
  B. Omission of important words
  C. Chapter and page identification

20. In the case of severe storms, the plane will be grounded.
  A. Adverb clause
  B. Verbal phrase
  C. Prepositional phrase

21. Speed and accuracy can be increased by determination, practice, and hard work.
  A. Phrases in a series
  B. Words in a series
  C. Clauses in a series

22. Our original investment, a very substantial sum, has shown a creditable profit.
  A. A nonrestrictive appositive
  B. An "of phrase" that follows a name
  C. An abbreviation that follows a name

23. As the manager walked into the room, he knew something was wrong.
  A. Adverb clause
  B. Transitional phrase
  C. Nominative absolute

24. Mr. Smith, can the decision be reversed?
  A. Interrupts the flow
  B. Expresses a parenthetical thought
  C. A noun in direct address

25. Did the sales manager ask, "Who made this sale?"
  A. Clauses built on contrast
  B. Easily misread words
  C. Identification purposes

Part II

Identify the correct usage in the following sentences by placing a check mark before the correct answer.

26. To give added information to the reader, use
  A. Parentheses   B. Brackets

27. We need
    A. Two-thirds of the vote   B. Two thirds of the vote

28. He owns a
    A. 16-foot sailboat   B. 16 feet sailboat

29. It is now nine
    A. o clock   B. o'clock

30. I
    A. haven't decided yet   B. have'nt decided yet

31. To set off a parenthetical expression that is a complete sentence, use
    A. Parentheses   B. Brackets

32. To de-emphasize a nonrestrictive phrase, use
    A. Parentheses   B. Brackets

33. Next year I will turn
    A. forty-four   B. forty four

34. This will be a
    A. four-week project   B. four weeks' project

35. To surround the word <u>sic</u>, use
    A. Parentheses   B. Brackets

Part III

Indicate whether the statement is true or false by placing a T or an F after the number.

36. Titles of major literary works usually appear in italics or underlines.

37. A semicolon is used to separate independent clauses not joined by a comma and a coordinate conjunction.

38. Identical verbs in a sentence are separated by commas.

39. Parenthetical expressions that are complete sentences are never punctuated as such.

40. Spell out isolated numbers from <u>one</u> to <u>ten</u>.

41. Spell out all ordinal numbers.

42. A question mark, exclamation mark, or a dash can appear inside or outside a closing quotation mark.

43. Introductory elements are usually followed by a semicolon.

44. Use commas to separate items in an address when that address is written <u>in-line</u>.

45. Never put a mark of punctuation such as a question mark or exclamation mark within a parentheses by itself.

46. Write out the shorter of two consecutive numbers if no punctuation mark intervenes.
47. When two numbers occur together and both are words or both are figures, separate them with commas.
48. An indirect quotation is always set off by quotation marks.
49. A conjunctive adverb is a description of the placement of a parenthetical adverb next to the semicolon joining two independent clauses.
50. Use commas to separate items in a date.
51. Brackets are only used within a parentheses.
52. The word sic means "thus," and indicates that the author is being quoted exactly.
53. Parentheses are used to enclose numbers or letters that identify items that appear in-line in series.
54. Consistency is necessary when expressing numbers in words or figures.
55. A colon is used after a formal introduction that includes or suggests words such as the following.
56. Expressions that begin with not, never, or seldom are set off by commas.
57. Periods and commas always appear inside the closing quotation mark.
58. Semicolons and colons always appear outside the closing quotation mark.
59. In some cases a semicolon can be a mark of elevation.
60. A colon is never used to separate two main clauses.

Part IV

Choose the letter that precedes the correct response.

61. (A) 40, (B) Forty, (C) Fourty leading production engineers visited the plant last week.
62. Good government is (A) everyones, (B) everyones', (C) everyone's concern.
63. The deliverymen have been here and (A) there, (B) they're, (C) their certain that the mistake has been corrected.
64. We owe a vote of gratitude to (A) our, (B) hour, (C) our's panel of experts.
65. (A) Your, (B) Your's, (C) You're truly an asset to the company.

66. All employees are eligible for a 20 percent discount on the price of (A) they're, (B) there, (C) their season tickets.

67. Jack Selby, (A) whose, (B) whos, (C) who's office this is, has agreed to the merger.

68. The package is (A) theres, (B) theirs, (C) their's.

69. Close the letter: (A) <u>your's</u>, (B) <u>Yours</u>, (C) <u>yours truly</u>.

70. This report is extremely clear in (A) its, (B) it's, (C) its' presentation of the facts.

Part V

Choose the correctly punctuated sentence in each group by placing a check mark before the appropriate choice.

71. A. These courses are required of all computer majors namely physics, math, and statistics.
   B. These courses are required of all computer majors; namely, physics, math, and statistics.
   C. These courses are required of all computer majors, namely, physics, math, and statistics.

72. A. The Southern California advertising agency of Bemis, Bormer, and Beard offers exceptional opportunities for employment as far south as San Diego.
   B. The southern California Advertising Agency of Bemis, Bormer, and Beard: offers exceptional opportunities for Employment as far South as San Diego.
   C. The Southern California Advertising Agency of Bemis, Bormer, and Beard offers exceptional opportunities for Employment as far south as San Diego.

73. A. When we saw the movie Ragtime we did not compare it with the book Ragtime by Doctorow.
   B. When we saw the movie "Ragtime," we did not compare it with the book Ragtime by Doctorow.
   C. When we saw the movie <u>Ragtime</u>, we did not compare it with the book <u>Ragtime</u> by Doctorow.

74. A. The new training class is 3/4 full.
   B. The new training class is three-fourths full.
   C. The new training class is three fourths full.

75. A. Debbie frequently spells <u>until</u> with two l's, but that spelling is incorrect.
   B. Debbie frequently spells until with two ls but that spelling is incorrect.
   C. Debbie frequently spells until with two ls, but that spelling is incorrect.

76. A. This building is scheduled for demolition beginning June 15 the new building <u>moreover</u> is not scheduled for completion until June 1985.
    B. This building is scheduled for demolition beginning June 15; the new building, moreover, is not scheduled for completion until June 1985.
    C. This building is scheduled for demolition beginning June 15 the new building; moreover, is not scheduled for completion until June 1985.

77. A. Three competing agencies Jay Walker Brown & Little and Millers are submitting bids Thursday.
    B. Three competing agencies—Jay Walker, Brown & Little, and Millers—are submitting bids Thursday.
    C. Three competing agencies (Jay Walker Brown & Little and Millers) are submitting bids Thursday.

78. A. One half of the positions in our San Diego office are filled by people with five years' experience.
    B. 1/2 of the positions in our San Diego office are filled by by people with 5 years experience.
    C. One-half of the positions in our Sand Diego office are filled people with 5 years experience.

79. A. The article stated The losses to four brokerage house sic are currently estimated at over $4 million.
    B. The article stated, "The losses to four brokerage house sic are currently estimated at over $4,000,000."
    C. The article stated, "The losses to four brokerage house [sic] are currently estimated at over $4 million."

80. A. The Medlock tool co.; appreciates the information received from the Corpus Christi board of Education on January 17.
    B. The Medlock Tool Co. appreciates the information received from the Corpus Christi Board of Education on January 17.
    C. The Medlock Tool Co. appreciates the information received from the Corpus Christi Board of Education on January 17.

81. A. Sander J. Caldwell has made over $1,000,000 in insurance.
    B. Sander J. Caldwell has made over a million dollars in insurance.
    C. Sander J. Caldwell has made over $1,000,000 in insurance.

82. A. He is still the No. 1 salesman at Haley, Inc..
    B. Is he still the No. 1 salesman at Haley Inc
    C. He is still the No. 1 salesman at Haley, Inc.

83. A. John was granted a 2 month leave.
    B. John was granted a two-month leave.
    C. John was granted a 2-month leave.

84. A. Why don't you travel to San Francisco along the coast up scenic Highway 1?
    B. Why don't you travel to San Francisco; up scenic Highway 1, along the coast?
    C. Why don't you travel to san Francisco up Scenic highway 1: along the coast.

85. A. Three fourths of our employees drive more than twenty minutes each way to work unfortunately we have no ride-sharing plan in effect.
    B. Three-fourths of our employees drive more than twenty minutes each way to work, unfortunately; we have no ride-sharing plan in effect.
    C. Three fourths of our employees drive more than twenty minutes each way to work; unfortunately, we have no ride-sharing plan in effect.

86. A. Was it Barbara McCauley who asked, "if the Executive club was for men only"?
    B. Was it Barbara McCauley who asked if the Executive Club was for men only?
    C. Was it Barbara McCauley who asked" if the Executive Club was for men only?"

87. A. The managers was it at last Wednesday meeting? finally agreed to build an employees recreation hall.
    B. The managers (was it at last Wednesday's meeting?) finally agreed to build an employees recreation hall.
    C. The managers, was it at last Wednesdays meeting; finally agreed to build an employees recreation hall.

88. A. We are presently editing 5 technical manuals, 42 company handouts, and 17 brochures
    B. We are presently editing five technical manuals, forty-two company handouts, and 17 brochures.
    C. We are presently Editing five technical manuals, forty-two company handouts, and 17 brochures.

89. A. His resumé indicates that his four years in High School; and his two years in Community College were supported by part-time work at sears.
    B. His resumé indicates that his four years in high school and his two years in community college were supported by part-time work at Sears.
    C. His resumé indicates that his four years in High schol and his two years in Community college were supported by Part-time work at Sears.

90. A. Most visitors to Washington have one major stop in mind: the White House.

B. Most visitors to Washington have one Major Stop in mind: the White House.

C. Most visitors to Washington have one major stop in mind; the White House.

91. A. The Director of the Lakeland hotel is john Golis; jr.; the Assistant director is still Marion Freeman.

B. The Director of the Lakeland Hotel is John Golis, jr.; the Assistant director is still Marion Freeman.

C. The director of the Lakeland Hotel is John Golis, Jr.; the assistant director is still Marion Freeman.

92. A. We have in stock at this writing the following sizes A-9613 H9472 and J9823.

B. We have in stock, at this writing, the following sizes: A-9613, H-9472, and J-9823.

C. We have in stock at this writing the following sizes; A9,613, H9,472, and J9,823.

93. A. Reading your credentials, I find that you are exactly the person we have been looking for; can you start Monday?

B. Reading your credentials I find that you are exactly the person we have been looking for can you start Monday?

C. Reading your credentials; I find that you are exactly the person we have been looking for. Can you start Monday?

94. A. Is organizational ability really important for a mid-management position? asked Mrs. Elliott.

B. Is organizational ability really Important for a Mid-management position asked Mrs. Elliott.

C. "Is organizational ability really important for a mid-management position?" asked Mrs. Elliott.

95. A. The newspapers point of view which I do not share is that a secretary's contribution most often exceeds an employers.

B. The newspaper's point of view (which I do not share) is that a secretary's contribution most often exceeds an employer's.

C. The Newspapers' point of view (which I do not share) is that a secretarys' contribution most often exceeds an employers.

96. A. The sales tax on this item amounts to one dollar, and thirty two cents.

B. The sales tax on this item amounts to one dollar and thirty-two cents.

C. The sales tax on this item amounts to $1.32.

97. A. Roger interrupted us by saying, "Let me read you a quote from James C. Sanders, the new chief of the Small Business Administration, 'Few businesses can afford to borrow at current high interest rates.'"

   B. Roger interrupted us by saying Let me read you a quote from James C. Sanders the new chief of the Small Business Administration Few businesses can afford to borrow at current high interest rates.

   C. Roger interrupted us by saying, "Let me read you a quote from James C. Sanders, the new chief of the Small Business Administration Few businesses can afford to borrow at current high interest rates."

98. A. A Savings Account; however, draws exceptional Interest Rates at santa monica bank if a deposit is made before the 15th of each month.

   B. A savings account, however, draws exceptional interest rates at Santa Monica Bank if a deposit is made before the 15th of each month.

   C. A Savings Account, however; draws exceptional interest rates at Santa Monica bank if a deposit is made before the 15th of each month.

99. A. The missouri and mississippi rivers flow from North to south, the ohio river flows from east to west.

   B. The Missouri and Mississippi rivers flow from north to south; the Ohio River flows from east to west.

   C. The Missouri and Mississippi Rivers flow from North to South: the Ohio River flows from East to West.

100. A. If Miller & Miller's policy does not change, it will soon find itself without clients to represent.

   B. If Miller and Millers policy does not change they will soon find themselves without clients to represent.

   C. If Miller & Miller's policy does not change; it will soon find itself without clients' to represent.

Key Section

PRACTICE COMMA RULE 1

1. The new house, as a consequence, cannot be sold for six months.

2. If you change your mind, Harry, please call.

3. The front window, obviously broken, was of little use.

4. We were all given, although we did not know the reason, the day off next Monday.

5. We had a meeting with Thomas B. Harding, of Washington, last week.

6. We hired Joseph Deerling, Ph.D., as a consultant last June.

7. I visited Mary, whom you have never met, last weekend.

8. Mr. Smith, our treasurer, read the quarterly report at the annual stockholders' meeting.

1. ___C___

2. ___D___

3. ___B___

4. ___A___

5. ___G___

6. ___F___

7. ___A___

8. ___E___

119

9. The new drapes, we all agreed, were worth the long wait.

9. _C_

10. March Bros., Inc., has just opened a new office in our building.

10. _F_

11. Many people, as you know, have come forward to offer Jane help and encouragement.

11. _C_

12. You will find, Mr. Smith, that your account has been adjusted and your balance corrected.

12. _D_

13. The Agony and the Ecstasy, which was written by Irving Stone, is a novel about Michelangelo.

13. _A_

14. Speaking to Janet Perkins, of Smith & Co., has caused Mr. Homes to change his mind about the merger.

14. _G_

15. Aunt Sis, a very distant but dear relative, is still one of my favorite people.

15. _E_

PRACTICE COMMA RULE 2

1. The vice-president spoke about personnel changes, improved equipment, and revised production schedules.

2. A simple, error-proof method for incorporating the Wang equipment into your organization is enclosed.

3. Endeavor to make your letter concise, specific, and clear.

4. The local drugstore sells office supplies, paper clips, pencils, pens, etc.[1] that we use on a daily basis.

5. This dress is old, old, old.

6. Watkins is looking for a permanent, challenging, secure position with a local bank.

7. The stationery store specializes in diplomas, certificates, memo pads, etc., for school or office.

8. Interviews will be held at 10:00 A.M., 1:30 P.M., and 3:00 P.M.

9. These forms may be used to record the sale of stocks, mortgages, and other securities.

10. Kathy looked under the table, on the shelf, and in the desk for the book.

11. The chair is made of wood and leather, has a firm texture, and is well suited to your office needs.

[1] The comma after etc. is optional. It depends on whether the items in the series are also seen as nonrestrictive appositives.

120

12. The new extensions assigned to the office are 7264, 7265, and 7266.

13. When you come home from the conference, I want you to do the dishes, fold the clothes, and make the beds.

14. In recent months Bob has sold his house, bought a new car, and moved into a bachelor apartment.

15. The booklet tells you why, where, and how modern office procedures developed.

PRACTICE COMMA RULE 3

Example: Mary sings in the choir, but John only listens.

1. The dictionary employs a uniform system of marking, yet people sometimes have trouble pronouncing certain words.

2. John has decided not to attend the convention, nor will he help organize any pre-convention activities.

3. We discussed the matter with Ms. Shipley and Mr. Lester, and they have promised to have the material delivered by March 15.

4. I have decided to stay late today, so you may take the afternoon off.

5. We are shipping the material immediately, and you may expect it within a week or ten days.

6. You need to make a payment by the tenth of the month, or you will have to pay a penalty again.

7. John has promised to fill out the enclosed form and mail it to us by Friday.[2]

8. Ms. Drake expects to receive the new catalogs from the printer today and will mail you a copy within the week.

9. The canvass was made in the neighborhood of Oak Avenue, Elm Avenue, Pine Avenue, and Walnut Avenue, and the results were predictable.

10. We steadfastly maintain our innocence, for we are the oldest and most reputable real estate brokerage firm in the South Bay Area.

[2]This sentence has one subject/verb core. The infinitives to fill and to mail are being coordinated. No comma is needed before the coordinate conjunction.

11. A Southern California Edison <u>crew</u> <u>is working</u> hard to repair the damage, and <u>we</u> <u>hope</u> to have your power restored by 3:30 P.M. today.

12. This vacation <u>package</u> <u>allows</u> you to enjoy Italy, Germany, and France in a series of little trips, or <u>you</u> <u>can choose</u> one country and <u>enjoy</u> its attractions fully.[3]

13. Our <u>responsibility</u> <u>was called</u> into question, so <u>we</u> <u>could take</u> no further action.

14. <u>We</u> <u>thought</u> the investigation was closed, yet <u>we</u> <u>ordered</u> a thorough study of processes, materials, and prices.

15. <u>It</u> <u>is</u> always better to specify the exact time of arrival, so there <u>can be</u> no uncertainty.

PRACTICE COMMA RULE 4

1. In making his selection, the manager interviewed three different applicants for the position.
2. As I previously told you, the meeting will take place a week from this Friday.
3. Because the money has not been appropriated by Congress, the program is being shut down.
4. To accommodate my boss, I took my vacation in July.
5. The work being already underway, it was impossible not to sustain a loss.
6. Wow, I just found out I'm going to be promoted.
7. On the other hand, it could be that the new comptroller just needs to relax a bit.
8. Having spent several years with that company, Tom feels he's now an expert in hydrolic engineering.
9. In the pocket of the purse at the bottom of the basket was $1,000.
10. On Friday we will meet the new manager.
11. Surprised by the interruption, Mr. Sellers tried to act non-committal.
12. As every person who applied was unacceptable, Mr. March is running the ad for another week.
13. Before long, day seems like night if you are living in Alaska.

---

[3]The coordinate conjunction <u>or</u> joins the two independent clauses. The coordinate conjunction <u>and</u> joins two verbs.

14. If taxes have to be increased before the end of the year, the country will certainly suffer.
15. Since no one else seems willing, I will come in on Friday to do the proofreading.

PRACTICE COMMA RULE 5

1. The longer I worked, the more confident I became.
2. Ted Baxter is the president of E.M.I., isn't he?
3. The weekly sales meeting usually runs for a full two hours, seldom longer.
4. Most people who vote, vote out of concern for the democratic processes.
5. Although majestic, Pikes Peak is more inspiring to look at than to climb.
6. To promote sales, campaigns should be developed with the user in mind.
7. The longer Mr. Jones waited, the more irritated he became.
8. The fall sale will be held November 19, not November 20.
9. John is going to the conference, is he not?
10. In Susan, Harris has found a secretary who is dependable, imaginative, and capable.
11. The longer the meeting lasted, the more heated the discussion became.
12. The people who will work, work long and hard.
13. You're going to the conference, aren't you?
14. Management sometimes works on Saturday.
15. To increase our sales, staff and management alike must make a concerted effort.

PRACTICE COMMA RULE 6

1. The proposal stated, "Further testing of the product is necessary."
2. "Tell no one about the proposed merger," the vice president cautioned, "even though you might be tempted to do so."
3. The First-Place winner will receive $1,000; second place, $700; and third place, $500.
4. The salesman replied, "The word processor is essential for the office of the future."

5. You will find the cited material in Chapter 4, page 47; Chapter 8, page 107; and Chapter 12, page 272.

6. The president implied that the company was interested in a merger.

7. "Competition is what makes used-car sales a challenge," concluded the sales manager.

8. Mr. Wallis said, "Individual interviews are a necessary part of placement."

9. "The Exalon Company is proud of its reputation," the letter said, "and we expect our customers to be equally satisfied."

10. "I have here," the shop foreman retorted, "facts and figures that prove your report is wrong."

11. The manager asked, "Is anybody in charge here?"

12. Did the manager ask, "Is anybody in charge here?"

13. Did the manager ask about who was "responsible"?

14. Last week, Ms. Kingsley made three important personnel changes; this week, two more.

15. The manager said, "The staff deserves special recognition"; however, nothing further seemed to be done.[4]

PRACTICE COMMA RULE 7

Part A

1. There were 7,583 people at the conference in Forth Worth.   1. __C__

2. The merchandise you ordered on February 9, 1982, was shipped to Evergreen, Ltd., 279 W. Olympic Blvd., Gig Harbor, WA 90266, on February 10.   2. __A__

3. We will be looking forward to the meeting on Thursday May 9, 1982, at the Ramada Inn.   3. __B__

4. We shipped Invoice 7256 on July 7, 1981.   4. __C & B__

5. On March 11, 1979, the telephone company celebrated its fifteenth anniversary.   5. __B__

[4]Two alternatives: (1) The manager said, "The staff deserves special recognition; however, nothing further seemed to be done." (2) The manager said, "The staff deserves special recognition"; however, nothing further seemed to be done.

6. Mark C. Bloom is located at 1117 Western Ave., Los Angeles, California.

6. ___A___

7. If all goes well, our vacation will begin on May 17, 1982, and will not end until August 3, 1982.

7. ___B___

8. The company has purchased the old Wheatfield Building at 472 Longview, Costa Mesa, California.

8. ___A___

9. There were more than 1,473 participants in the audience for the March 3, 1982, Association presentation.

9. ___B & C___

10. The meeting will be held in May 1983, not March 1983.

10. ___B___

Part B

Smith, Thomas
Ulack, Joyce
Speed, Patricia
Holmes, John
Wise, Buyonne

Part C

Respectfully,
Respectfully yours,
Sincerely,
Yours truly,
Regards,

PRACTICE SEMICOLON RULES

1. The allowable discounts are suggested in the enclosed brochure; i.e., 20 to 30 percent of all discontinued stock.[5]

1. ___C___

2. Mr. Jones, you have ignored our polite reminder regarding your overdue account; actually, this is not the first time you have done this.

2. ___A___

[5]The difference between a semicolon being used to separate independent clauses and a semicolon being used to introduce examples is the examples are usually not a complete clause.

3. Pete Lundy's itinerary includes San Diego, California; Portland, Oregon; and Seattle, Washington.

3. ___B___

4. Please let us know your decision immediately; we'd like to begin the sales campaign as soon as possible.

4. ___A___

5. The first edition went into print two years ago; the second edition will be out in three months.

5. ___A___

6. Several items need to be examined more carefully; for example, cost-accounting procedures and the year-end report.

6. ___C___

7. I suppose it's better to work until 5:00 P.M. every day; still I'm always ready to go home by 4:00 P.M.

7. ___A___

8. Renee will program the computer while Carole checks the previous printout; that way, the problem will be solved more quickly.

8. ___A___

9. People fear that the word processor will cost them jobs; it was never designed to reduce the labor force.

9. ___A___

10. Mary resembles her father; Debbie looks like her mother.

10. ___A___

11. The new plants will be located on the outskirts of Dallas, Texas; Phoenix, Arizona; and Tulsa, Oklahoma.

11. ___B___

12. The decision to move the office, which had been in the same location for twenty years, was made suddenly; but the overall result has been beneficial.[6]

12. ___B___

13. The office manager is responsible for all the equipment; namely, desks, typewriters, and calculators.

13. ___C___

14. These statistics were excluded in the first draft; please add them to your present edition.

14. ___A___

15. Both individuals come with excellent recommendations; however, we can hire only one engineer.

15. ___A___

[6]You wouldn't be wrong if you put a comma before <u>but</u>.

PRACTICE COLON RULES

1. The plane leaves LAX at 4:15 this afternoon.

    1. __C__

2. Please buy the following at the stationer's:
   note pads
   paper clips
   desk calendars

    2. __A__

3. The manager had only one recourse: to fire the secretary.

    3. __A__

4. The letter served its purpose: It saved the account.

    4. __B__

5. Remember this: A fool and his money are soon parted.

    5. __A or B__

6. This accounting procedure has two advantages: it reduces errors and saves money.

    6. __A or B__

7. The office was exactly what we wanted: affordable, yet large.

    7. __A__

8. The meeting has been changed from 1:30 to 3:45 this afternoon.

    8. __C__

9. Dear Mr. Sellers:

    9. __C__

10. Mark Twain wrote: "A powerful agent is the right word, whenever we come upon one of those intensely right words in a book or a newspaper the resulting effect is physical as well as spiritual, and electrically prompt."

    10. __A__

11. Ms. Davis recently ordered the following furniture for her new office: three desks, six chairs, two sofas, two IBM Selectrics, one calculator, and one adding machine.

    11. __A__

12. Our new advertising campaign will be directed towards economy car buyers: It will stress mileage maintenance and reliability.

    12. __B__

13. The sales meeting begins at 9:30 and usually lasts until 11:00 each Tuesday.

    13. __C__

14. The office uses several different kinds of typewriters: IBM, Olivetti, Olympia.

    14. __A__

15. Dear Mr. Postmaster General:

    15. __C__

PRACTICE DASH RULES

1. This course of action—as our accountant maintains—will save the company a half-million dollars a year.

    1. ___A___

2. The manager has only one goal—retirement.

    2. ___B___

3. Experience qualification and excellent references—all are essential to getting a good job.

    3. ___B___

4. Every manager—and you're no exception—is responsible for a department's budget.

    4. ___A___

5. Mr. Baysworth requested the information—information needed to complete the quarterly report.

    5. ___C___

6. We already have branch offices in several states—Texas, Oregon, Washington, and Nevada—that are operating at a loss.

    6. ___A___

7. The problem is simply solved—for example, personnel evaluations need to be updated.

    7. ___A___

8. If there are any problems, phone—no, come in as soon as possible to discuss your tax situation.

    8. ___B___

9. Labor, equipment, and time—those are the major concerns in remodeling.

    9. ___B___

10. The experience—difficult and painful as it may be—should prove profitable.

    10. __A or C__

11. Thanksgiving, Christmas, New Year's—these are the only official company holidays.

    11. ___B___

12. Additional road equipment—a bulldozer, a backhoe, and a grader—was needed to complete the contract.

    12. ___A___

13. We expect perhaps—oh, about a 15 percent reduction in staff this year.

    13. ___B___

14. Negotiations—after reaching an impasse on June 10—were resumed on July 1.

    14. ___A___

15. Our sales—overall sales—have increased by 15 percent since the end of the fiscal year.

    15. ___A___

PRACTICE HYPHEN RULES

1. Inspection will begin on ten-, twenty-, and thirty-story buildings the first of next month.
2. These forms should be filled in by Monday.
3. The filled-in forms should be returned by Monday.
4. Three fourths of this year's profits has already been reinvested.
5. A three-fourths majority is needed to reinvest the money.
6. The selfish manager considered himself to be self-made.
7. This store carries the finest quality goods.
8. This is only a three-year contract.
9. The contract lasts only three years.
10. Thomas Coswell is a well-known public speaker.
11. The ex-football player is now in the insurance business.
12. This business was started by my great-grandfather.
13. A certain well-known executive has changed jobs four times in a five-year period.
14. This building offers one-, three-, and five-year lease options.

PRACTICE PARENTHESES RULES

1. Management has already embarked upon cost-saving budget reduction (see attached supplement).
2. This sale (it's our going-out-of-business sale) is too good to miss.
3. The department meeting served to (1) improve communication, (2) increase quality standards, and (3) develop rapport between management and staff.
4. There is no possibility (?) that the budget will be approved as written.
5. The normal fee for our service totals seven hundred dollars ($700), payable by check or VISA.
6. Our representative Mr. Paul Sloane (didn't you meet him at the Atlanta Conference?) will be stopping by your office next Monday.
7. The Licensee hereby agrees to pay Licensor on the first day of each month, commencing on the first of January Nineteen hundred eighty-three, the sum of five hundred dollars ($500).
8. (Punctuate a separate sentence) Please compare our product with others on the market. (This month's issue of <u>Newsweek</u> has several excellent ads.)

9. The assistant director (I believe his name is John Thornton) has not returned my calls.[7]

10. The United Nations has several objectives: (A) world understanding, (B) world communication, and (C) world peace.

11. You have already learned (see Chapter 1) that financing for this project is dependent on government approval.

12. We need the representative (if he ever gets here) to answer our questions.

13. If you follow my suggestion (and you should), you will reconsider your decision.

14. Go by yourself (you can do it on company time), and I will sign the authorization.

15. This price was high ($1,975), but worth it.

PRACTICE QUOTATION MARKS RULE 1

1. Maria Huffner said, "We anticipate a 3 percent return of merchandise."

2. "A 3 percent return of merchandise," said Maria Huffner, "is anticipated."

3. "A 3 percent return of merchandise is anticipated," said Maria Huffner.

4. Maria Huffner said that a 3 percent return of merchandise is anticipated.

5. The report stated, "According to Maria Huffner, 'A 3 percent return of merchandise is anticipated.'"

6. Dr. Roger Wilson predicted that the economy will begin to stabilize by next year.

7. "The economy," suggested Dr. Roger Wilson, "will begin to stabilize by next year."

8. "The economy will begin to stabilize by next year," suggested Dr. Roger Wilson.

9. Dr. Roger Wilson suggested the economy will begin to stabilize by next year.

10. The newspaper article stated, "According to Dr. Roger Wilson, 'The economy will begin to stabilize by next year.'"

11. The newspaper predicts that it will be impossible to meet the deadline.

[7]Alternate punctuation: The assistant director (I believe his name is John Thornton?) has not returned my calls.

130

12. The newspaper quoted a <u>Newsweek</u> article by the Secretary of State, "It will be impossible to meet the deadline."

13. The Secretary of State suggested, "It will be impossible to meet the deadline."

14. "It will be impossible," said the Secretary of State, "to meet the deadline."

15. "It will be impossible to meet the deadline," said the Secretary of State.

PRACTICE QUOTATION MARK AND ELLIPSIS RULES

Part A

"Faith of Our Fathers"
(address by John Foster Dulles)

<u>The Yearbook of Labor Statistics</u>

<u>The American Commonwealth</u>
(book) by Viscount James Bryce

<u>The Crisis of the Old Order</u>
(book) by Arthur N. Schlesinger, Jr.

"Area Production of Principle Crops" (report)

<u>Who's Who in America 1980</u>

<u>Wealth of Nations</u>
(book) by Adam Smith

"All systems are go"

<u>The Theory of the Leisure Class</u>
(book) by Thorstein Veblen

Part B

1. There were at least ten executives attending the conference: Allen P. Havier . . . John Hershey.

2. Successive quotations in one paragraph may usually be documented in a single note. . . .

3. The home office is separated from its ten branches: Houston . . . Phoenix?

4. Please ship the order by November 14 or. . . .

5. All good men must. . . .

PRACTICE APOSTROPHE RULES

SINGULAR	SINGULAR POSSESSIVE	PLURAL	PLURAL POSSESSIVE
1. stockholder	stockholder's	stockholders	stockholders'
2. everybody[8]	everybody's		
3. life	life's	lives	lives'

[8]There is no plural form.

SINGULAR	SINGULAR POSSESSIVE	PLURAL	PLURAL POSSESSIVE
4. letterhead	letterhead's	letterheads	letterheads'
5. I[9]	my, mine	we	our, ours
6. brother-in-law	brother-in-law's	brothers-in-law	brothers-in-law's
7. ox	ox's	oxen	oxen's
8. party	party's	parties	parties'
9. attorney general	attorney general's	attorneys general	attorneys general's
10. woman	woman's	women	women's
11. radio	radio's	radios	radios'
12. Brown & Brown[10]	Brown & Brown's		
13. tax	tax's	taxes	taxes'
14. Adams	Adams' Adams's	Adamses	Adamses'
15. committee	committee's	committees	committees'
16. county	county's	counties	counties'
17. month	month's	months	months'
18. journey	journey's	journeys	journeys'
19. anyone[11]	anyone's		
20. boss	boss's	bosses	bosses'

PRACTICE APOSTROPHE RULES

1. Ph.D. _Ph.D.'s_
2. etc. _etc.'s_
3. 5 _5's_
4. 1800 _1800s_
5. s _s's_
6. 100 _100's_
7. Terry _Terrys_
8. M.D. _M.D.'s_
9. 1960 _1960s_
10. SOS _SOS's_
11. CIA _CIA's, C.I.A.'s_
12. * _*'s_
13. t _t's_
14. C.O.D. _C.O.D.'s_

[9] Singular Possessive: my, mine
Plural: we
Plural Possessive: our, ours
[10] There is no plural form.
[11] There is no plural form.

15.	Susan _Susans_	18.	IOU _IOU's_
16.	Ellen _Ellens_	19.	L _L's_
17.	27 _27's_	20.	no _no's_

1.	of the clock _o'clock_	11.	who is _who's_
2.	would not _wouldn't_	12.	there has _there's_
3.	should not _shouldn't_	13.	does not _doesn't_
4.	they are _they're_	14.	cannot _can't_
5.	we will _we'll_	15.	she shall _she'll_
6.	you would _you'd_	16.	I will _I'll_
7.	I am _I'm_	17.	you had _you'd_
8.	it has _it's_	18.	she has _she's_
9.	I have _I've_	19.	he will _he'll_
10.	it is _it's_	20.	I had _I'd_

PRACTICE NUMBERS RULE 1

1. The 4 magazines were mailed to you on July 6.

   1. _four_

2. Write to the manufacturer at 1286 Twenty-third Street, Reston, VA 22090

   2. _23rd_

3. 6 leading production engineers visited the plant last Thursday.

   3. _six_

4. The American Patent Office receives well over 1,000,000 new patent applications a year.

   4. _one million_

5. Advertising accounts for over 1/4 of the nonmanufacturing cost.

   5. _one fourth_

6. We have 6 project managers; of the 6, 5 are college graduates.

   6. _six; six, five_

7. The new training class is 3/4 full.

   7. _three-fourths_

8. We have prepared thirty thousand 2-page brochures advertising our new product.

   8. _30,000 two-page_

9. This is the 10th annual convention.

   9. _tenth_

10. John was granted a 2-month leave of absence.

10. __two-month__

11. We're expecting about 50 people at the conference

11. __fifty__

12. Did you know that 5 of our copyrights have already expired?

12. __five__

13. The seminar begins tomorrow morning at 8 o'clock

13. __eight__

14. We need 42 12-inch rulers to finish the project.

14. __twelve-inch__

15. Mr. Jones, our president, has made Aerospace 1 of the most influential companies in the South Bay Area.

15. __one__

PRACTICE NUMBERS RULE 2

1. We have twenty-four male and female engineers on our staff at present.

1. __24__

2. Our magazine first appeared on the racks in nineteen sixty-four.

2. __1964__

3. His plane is due to arrive at LAX at five P.M.

3. __5:00__

4. In 1980, 13 of our original employees retired.

4. __thirteen__

5. We are manufacturing one thousand two hundred rockets an hour at this point.

5. __1,200__

6. We are presently editing five technical manuals, 42 company handouts, and 17 brochures.

6. __5__

7. The sales tax on this item amounts to one dollar and thirty-two cents.

7. __$1.32__

8. There were 72 engineers who attended the conference. Of the 72 59 attended the banquet Friday night.

8. __72, 59__

9. There are only 3 500-page reports left to do.

9. __three__

10. The Company Store usually gives twenty percent discounts on items purchased.

10. __20__

11. The stock closed at seven and a half.

11. __7½__

12. The president of our company lives just around the corner at 1993 Seventy-first street.

12. <u>71st</u>

13. Our accountant appeared on the news on Channel <u>Five</u> last night.

13. <u>5</u>

14. The temperature registered <u>forty-two</u> degrees Fahrenheit in mid-May.

14. <u>42</u>

15. The S. L. Strong Co. paid over <u>$5,000,000</u> for its new building.

15. <u>$5 million</u>

PRACTICE CAPITALS RULES

1. please meet tom at the corner of marine drive and elm street tuesday at noon.

1. <u>7</u>

2. After Lunch margie inquired, "do you want me to file the Correspondence, or should i wait?"

2. <u>5</u>

3. During the next Stockholders' meeting, president Chambers will introduce the new Vice President.

3. <u>4</u>

4. on saturday we had french toast, and on sunday we had omelettes.

4. <u>3</u>

5. Although he had lived in the east for many years, last winter he finally returned to miami.

5. <u>2</u>

6. The Company's labor day Picnic will be held a week from saturday at disneyland.

6. <u>6</u>

7. Mr. john Smith of the department of the interior will deliver an address next tuesday entitled, "appreciating the national park system."

7. <u>8</u>

8. The smithsonian institute, located in washington, d. c., is closed once a year, on christmas day.

8. <u>7</u>

9. In desperation mary retorted, "i am a Twenty-four-year-old catholic caucasian of irish descent, and i speak both spanish and french fluently. Would you like my Social Security number also."

9. <u>10</u>

10. Here is Kathy Holman's Address: 2472 Maryland pkw., battle creek, Michigan 59106.

10. <u>4</u>

135

11. The Manager's flight is booked on western airlines flight 402 leaving at 8:15 A.M. on monday.

11. __5__

12. the social security administration is responsible for sending my Mother her Monthly retirement check.

12. __6__

13. Now that you've met Mother, i would like You to meet my Cousin Barbara.

13. __3__

14. In the spring, it's hard for a student to concentrate on English and history.

14. __C__

15. The vice-president of the College, William J. Watson, ph.d., introduced president Jocelyn Simon to the Student Body.

15. __6__

PRACTICE PERIOD RULES

1. Ask for Mr. Strong.
2. The new letterhead stationery has been approved.
3. A common computer language used in business is called COBOL.
4. The clerk did not indicate that the price is now $478 a pair.
5. The 55 mph speed limit is strictly enforced by the CHP.[12]
6. The office has two CPA's: A. M. Butler and B. Jeff Sholls.
7. Our representative in Fresno is C. K. Bailey of S. Oakland St.
8. Mr. Sterman has worked for Henry H. Case Co., Inc., and Booth & Booth, Ltd.
9. Mr. F. H. Boreman has just been named president of the AAA of Southern California.[13]
10. Dr. T. F. Williams and Prof. Wadsworth will address a Westinghouse Symposium next Saturday, May 7.
11. Choose the color you want.
12. No, I won't.[14]
13. Will you please sit down.
14. Prof. Stetson asked the students if they had registered their complaints officially.
15. May I have a copy of last month's invoice.

[12]Optional: . . .C.H.P. (Never use two periods to end a sentence.)
[13]Optional: A.A.A.
[14]Optional: No. I won't.

PRACTICE QUESTION MARK AND EXCLAMATION POINT RULES

1. Look! There's your flight taking off right now.
2. Will you pay the bill this week, or next?
3. You did take messages while I was away from my desk?
4. Wait!
5. I can't believe it!
6. Bill Stroop (have you met him?) visited the branch offices last week.
7. Where were you in 1962? 1972? 1982?
8. Tom was wearing his new Botany 100(?) suit.
9. Although you're busy, will you be able to get the report out by noon?
10. May I hear from you by return mail.
11. Wonderful!
12. He asked me if I would be at the meeting.
13. Should we hold the meeting on Tuesday? Wednesday? Thursday?
14. Do you intend to change jobs?
15. What a beautiful day!

REVIEW EXERCISE #1

Part A   Score _____

1. The situation, since you asked, has always been the same.   1. _ADV._

2. The manager, whom you just met, is my immediate superior.   2. _ADJ._

3. George, who loves a good laugh, decided not to press the issue.   3. _ADJ._

4. Tricia Whitoff, whom we have decided to support in the next election, is a Democratic candidate.   4. _ADJ._

5. The sample were in the mail, as you requested, by last Tuesday.   5. _ADV._

(10 points)

Part B

1. You understand that, as a rule, we seldom make an exception.[15]

2. Ms. Ellen, obviously disturbed by the news, decided to go home early.

3. These shoes on display, Mrs. Jones, are our last pair on sale.

4. The need for an older manager, on the other hand, is obvious.

5. Mr. Jones just stood there, his eyes focused inward, after he heard that the union was really going on strike.

6. The new manager, however, seemed quite relieved by the news.

7. Can the decision, Mr. Smith, be reversed?

1. __A or B__

2. ___A___

3. ___C___

4. ___B___

5. ___A___

6. ___B___

7. ___C___

(14 points)

Part C

1. Shelly Adkins, my new manager, is from the Pacific Northwest.

2. The Sanfran Corporation, of Texas, has just opened new offices in Century City.

3. The company has been managed by Jerry Scott, Ph.D., and Thelma Tolbert, M.A., for the past three years.

4. Our original investment, a very substantial sum, has shown a creditable profit.

5. Although Steve Webber has his Ed.D. degree, he feels that he must prove himself to people like Thomas Starkly, Ph.D.

1. ___C___

2. ___B___

3. ___A___

4. ___C___

5. ___A___

(10 points)

[15]It is true that a parenthetical expression interrupts the flow, but not everything that interrupts the flow is parenthetical. Either A or B could be considered correct.

Part D

1. As the manager walked into the room, he knew something was wrong.

    1. __A__

2. Gee, Tom seemed upset.

    2. __E__

3. The story having already been told, progress seemed relatively slow.

    3. __D__

4. On the other hand, new materials were arriving daily.[16]

    4. __B__

5. To assure quality control, Tom checked each order personally.

    5. __C__

6. Because I have been so pleased with the product, I have not interviewed any other firm.

    6. __A__

7. In the case of severe storms, the plane will be grounded.

    7. __F__

8. By turning around quite slowly, Sue was able to catch the shoplifter in the act.

    8. __C__

9. In the meantime, the shop has been losing money.

    9. __B__

10. If the case were not so self-evident, I could change my opinion.

    10. __A__

(20 points)

Part E

1. The Sovereign Insurance Co. has district offices in Seattle, Portland, and Los Angeles.

    1. __A__

2. Jerry Toleman developed the idea, Susan Sands wrote the copy, and Tom Smith edited the final draft.

    2. __C__

3. Lucy looked in the drawer, under the desk, and behind the file cabinet for the missing documents.

    3. __B__

4. Terry Kreutzer is an assertive, self-reliant young executive.

    4. __D__

5. The 4th, 5th, and 6th floors are being remodeled this month.

    5. __A__

[16]The phrase on the other hand is a prepositional phrase, but it is much more transitional in meaning. However, either B or F would be correct.

6. The new manager strolled into the typing room, paused by the supervisor's desk, and casually asked who was in charge.[17]

6. ___A or B___

7. The early-morning, late-night schedules need to be changed.

7. ___D___

8. Speed and accuracy can be increased by determination, practice, and hard work.

8. ___A___

(16 points)

Part F

1. Whether or not you agree, John Russell has decided to resign his job, sell his home, and move to the Pacific Northwest.

2. I guess these are the last of the sale curtains, Mrs. Evers.

3. To become better acquainted with Sam Johnson, of Washington, we need to carry on an extensive correspondence with him.

4. All things being equal, my boss, Dr. Blythn, is usually a fair, impartial judge.

5. Sally is my favorite salesperson, but she needs to do something about her tendency to work, work, work.

6. Are you fully protected, Mr. Flood, against theft, injury, or accidental death?

7. Joyce Ulack decided to attend the banquet, but she could not find a ride.

8. Linda Campbell, D.D.S., has decided, I believe, to devote her spare time to a community reorganization project.

9. After she heard the good news, Ms. Kingsley just stood there for several minutes, her eyes closed in silent prayer.

10. Picking up the pace, the lead runner proceeded to set a new world's record.

11. If you had only asked, Mr. Smith, the outcome might have been different.[18]

12. H. L. Wheeler & Sons, a local company, has spent many hours researching that question.

[17]While these are, strictly speaking, verbs (words) in a series, there would be some justification for seeing them as verb phrases in a series. Therefore, either A or B would be correct.

[18]This sentence can be punctuated in two ways: (1) If you had only asked Mr. Smith, the outcome might have been different. (Addressing Mr. Smith) (2) If you had only asked, Mr. Smith, the outcome might have been different. (Introductory adverb clause speaking about Mr. Smith)

13. The awards went to Richard Dowing, Ph.D.; Phyllis Reynoso, Ed.D.; and Bennet Wood, M.D.

14. The <u>Los Angeles Times</u>, which is a morning paper, is responsible for researching and printing the morning news.

15. Do not, John, start work until you have developed a reasonable plan.

REVIEW EXERCISE #2

Part A   Score _____

1. Expressions that begin with <u>not</u>, <u>never</u>, or <u>seldom</u> are set off by commas.

   1. <u>Yes</u>

2. Commas are never used for identification purposes.

   2. <u>No</u>

3. Questions appended to preceding statements are set off by commas.

   3. <u>Yes</u>

4. Use commas to separate items in a date.

   4. <u>Yes</u>

5. Use commas to separate items in an address when that address is written <u>in-line</u>.

   5. <u>Yes</u>

6. There are never special usages for comma placement.

   6. <u>No</u>

7. Count numbers are separated by commas.

   7. <u>Yes</u>

8. Identification numbers are separated by commas.

   8. <u>No</u>

9. Identical verbs in a sentence are separated by commas.

   9. <u>Yes</u>

10. Commas are used to prevent misreading.

    10. <u>Yes</u>

(10 points)

Part B

1. In the fall, sale items are available.

   1. <u>A</u>

2. "The budget is being reviewed," responded the general manager, "and a decision should be forthcoming."

   2. <u>B</u>

3. The longer the meeting lasted, the sleepier I became.

3. ___D___

4. There are 4,523 cartons in this shipment alone.

4. ___C___

5. Mr. Garnet announced, "This Friday is a holiday."

5. ___B___

6. The more I pressed the issue, the more negative Mr. Styles became.

6. ___D___

7. At the hotel, business was slow.

7. ___A___

8. Did the sales manager ask, "Who made that sale?"

8. ___B___

9. "Who made the sale?" the sales manager asked.

9. ___B___

10. More than 1,483 delegates attended the conference.

10. ___C___

Part C

1. The monthly sales meeting will be held on Wednesday, not Friday.

1. ___A___

2. First prize for participation in this year's United Fund Campaign went to the Accounting Department; second prize, to Research and Development; and third prize, to Shipping.

2. ___D___

3. The reasons for promptness and courtesy are self-evident, are they not?

3. ___B___

4. Mrs. Stonewell's extension is 592, not 492.

5. ___A___

5. Last year's budget was $1,432, wasn't it?

5. ___B___

6. Every page in question has already been edited, hasn't it?

6. ___B___

7. Central Medical Group specializes in casualty insurance; Alliance, in health; and Webbco, in surety.

7. ___D___

8. By tomorrow's meeting read Chapter 7, page 42; Chapter 9, page 80; and Chapter 11, page 102.

8. ___C___

9. This committee was formed to reevaluate the proposal, wasn't it?

9. ___B___

10. The supervisor's report is due on June 15, not May 15.

10. ___A___

(20 Points)

Part D

1. The Richards whom you just met are not the Richards who were my next-door neighbors.

   1. ___B___

2. My car, which I really did not like, was finally sold.

   2. ___A___

3. Tom Smith, whom you have already met, is my friend.

   3. ___A___

4. I want to borrow your desk calculator after you are finished with it.

   4. ___D___

5. We decided, though it doesn't necessarily mean anything will be done, that the office needs new furniture.

   5. ___C___

6. We must go where the customers are.

   6. ___D___

7. The district manager, whom you have never met, will be visiting the office on Friday.

   7. ___A___

8. I will write a memo, although I can't guarantee the results.

   8. ___C___

9. The money that I spent is non-refundable.

   9. ___B___

10. The manager's office, which used to be mine, is now a conference room.

    10. ___A___

(20 points)

Part E

1. We had hoped that the Westwood Building would be completed by July, but rainy weather, strikes, and supply shortages have delayed the grand opening.

2. Working hard, he was able to meet the deadline.

3. To get to the root of the problem, you must make an appointment to see Mr. Tameron, not Mr. Jones.

4. "Profits," the chairman of the board repeated in a resigned voice, "have never been lower."

5. The current list reflects price increases, which were considered absolutely necessary.

6. The first offer on the building was $1.5 million; the second, $1.9 million.

7. The real estate committee compared condominium prices in Marina Del Rey, Venice, and Redondo Beach before making its recommendation.

8. Make sure, Mr. Jones, that everyone gets a copy of this report.

9. "This XYZ Stereo," cooed the salesman, "has a two-year, money-back guarantee."

10. As of March 15, 1982, our office is at its new location at 4423 Santa Monica Mall, Santa Monica, CA 90401.

11. Mr. Thompson, I believe, is in charge of ordering the paper, pencils, erasers, etc., needed in the office.

12. Prosperity, recession, depression, and recovery seem to be natural parts of a business cycle.

13. Equipment such as copiers, duplicators, and calculators is always ordered specially.

14. Merchants Bank, an early bond success of mine, has just opened its 14th branch office.

15. Our office should be fully automated by the year 1984.

(30 points)

REVIEW EXERCISE #3

Part A

1. A semicolon is used to separate independent clauses not joined by a comma and a coordinate conjunction.

1. Agree

2. In some cases a semicolon can be a mark of elevation.

2. Agree

3. A colon is never used to separate two main clauses.

3. Disagree

4. A colon is used after a formal introduction that includes or suggests words such as the following.

4. Agree

5. A conjunctive adverb is a name used to describe a parenthetical adverb that follows the semicolon joining two independent clauses.

5. Agree

6. A semicolon is used between items in a series when commas appear within the items.

6. Agree

7. Identical verbs in a sentence are separated by a comma.

7. Agree

144

8. Introductory elements are usually followed by a semicolon.

8. <u>Disagree</u>

9. Colons may be used to introduce a one-word appositive.

9. <u>Agree</u>

10. A colon is used to separate the hours from the minutes when recording time.

10. <u>Agree</u>

(20 points)

Part B

1. Walcott, Inc., shipped the new furniture two weeks ago; <u>however</u>, it was delayed in transit.

1. <u>A</u>

2. This building is scheduled to be demolished June 15; the new building, <u>moreover</u>, is not scheduled for completion until June 1985.

2. <u>C</u>

3. The plant will not be ready for production by October; <u>in other words</u>, we will be forced to delay the start of the new project.

3. <u>B</u>

4. We asked personnel to begin replacement proceedings for hiring another secretary; <u>hence</u> the ad in this morning's classified advertising section.

4. <u>A</u>

5. The purpose of the memo is to change the hiring policy; <u>in other words</u>, we want Mr. Sparyak to follow company policy more closely.

5. <u>B</u>

6. The decision was not easy; <u>on the other hand</u>, the choice was clear.

6. <u>B</u>

7. Mrs. Bentley has continuously ignored our requests; <u>obviously</u>, she does not intend to cooperate.

7. <u>A</u>

8. The production department has been severely cut back; the accounting department, <u>on the other hand</u>, has hired two new employees.

8. <u>C</u>

9. We asked you to delay the action; <u>in other words</u>, we want to reconsider the project.

9. <u>B</u>

10. Ms. Williams was not involved in the planning stage; <u>however</u>, she has been very active in production.

10. <u>A</u>

11. The sandwiches seemed stale; <u>otherwise</u>, it was a successful brunch.

11. <u>A</u>

12. Mrs. Wilson has been in advertising for the past four years; <u>actually</u>, her degree in Marketing has served her well in her career.

12. __A__

13. The wood paneling suits this office perfectly; the pink light fixture, <u>on the other hand</u>, seems to detract from the total effect.

13. __C__

14. Ed Jones is usually fair; <u>as a result</u>, the people who work for him admire him greatly.

14. __B__

15. The position has been filled already; <u>still</u>, you could submit a resumé.

15. __A__

(30 points)

Part C

about four in the afternoon	7:45 P.M.
Dear Ms. Wilson:	Dear Dr. Johnson:
Gentlemen:	12 midnight
To Whom It May Concern:	2:35 P.M.
7:18 A.M.	Dear Bishop Clark:

(10 points)

Part D

1. Write a sentence with a colon followed by one word.
   John has but one goal: retirement.
2. Write a sentence that uses a colon to introduce a list.
   We need the following: stationery, envelopes, black pens.
3. Write a sentence that introduces a list and does not use words such as namely or for example.
   The speakers include the following members: Mark Harkness, Sally Smith, and Susan Wilson.

(10 points)

Part E

1. In the morning the school is never open before 7:45 A.M.; however, it stays open every evening until 9:00 P.M.

2. A nurse may be trained at a hospital, a university, or both; a doctor, on the other hand, is always university trained.

3. College students should, I believe, make an effort to learn as much as possible, so they can apply their knowledge when they enter the labor force.[19]

4. Mr. Cross asked his assistant to telephone for a prompt, reliable, and trustworthy messenger.

5. By finding ways to cut down on unnecessary costs, the good manager demonstrates an interest in efficiency as well as cost-effectiveness.

6. An outgoing, warm personality is an asset to any person in business, but nothing takes the place of experience and knowledge.

7. The cleaning crew plan to wax the floor and clean the windows in the reception area next week; this week they will shampoo the rugs and wash down the walls.

8. The main problem with the new design is the cost; the solution, however, seems very near at hand.

9. We have in stock, at this writing, the following sizes: A9613, H9472, and J9823.[20]

10. Your suggestion, I'm sorry to say, came at a time when we had no budget allowance for new furniture; next year's budget should rectify that problem.

11. The Ajax Agency can always be counted on for one thing: creativity.

12. Ted, Bob, and Alice worked late four nights this week; moreover, they plan to spend at least Saturday afternoon completing the layout.

13. You might say, Mr. Merriweather, that the success of the project depends upon you.

14. This has not been Mr. Atkins' day: He arrived late for the executive meeting, broke his reading glasses, and tripped over Mr. Crump's briefcase.

15. Yes, Mr. Sandoval can meet with you today; however, he won't be free until after 2:30 this afternoon.

(30 points)

[19]The use of the semicolon before the coordinate conjunction so is optional. The writer may choose to use a comma.
[20]The use of the comma around at this writing is optional. However, you must use either two commas or no commas.

REVIEW EXERCISE #4

Part A

Score _____

1. The novel is never to be forgotten.

   never-to-be-forgotten novel

2. This extension is only for a short term.

   short-term extension

3. The museum specializes in paintings of the fifteenth century.

   fifteenth-century paintings

4. We cruised the harbor in a sailboat that was 16 feet long.

   16-foot-long sail boat

5. The manager looks friendly.

   friendly-looking manager

6. The budget estimate should be brought up to date.

   up-to-date budget estimate

7. The test should have every blank filled in.

   fill-in-the-blank test

8. There is a speed trap of 25 miles per hour close to the office.

   25-mile-per-hour speed trap

9. The beginning salary is $10,000 a year.

   $10,000-a-year salary

10. His next business trip will last three weeks.

    three-week business trip

(20 points)

Part B

1. Mr. Foinsworth has but one choice—success!

   1. ___C___

2. Several employees have worked for this firm for over fifteen years—for example, Kristen Kauffman, Linda Davis, and Mark Andrew.

   2. ___B___

3. I can't overstate the present need—cost control.

   3. ___C___

4. Our quarterly magazine—which you have contested—was recently discontinued.

   4. ___A___

5. Our new building—despite major setbacks—is finally ready for inspection.

   5. ___A___

6. The accounting department—as you well know—has had its ups and downs during the past year.

   6. ___A___

7. There's one item we forgot—the word processor.

   7. ___C___

8. The opposition by several committee members—namely, Steven Blumberg, Dave Walker, and Tom Lesser—was quite vocal.

8. ___B___

9. Mr. Jarvis did not consider an important factor—recession.

9. ___C___

10. These courses are required of all computer majors—namely, physics, math, and statistics.

10. ___B___

11. Mr. Strong's visit will convince you—we hope—that our company can handle your casualty line.

11. ___A___

12. That particular section of highway—which buckled in the heat—will take nine months to repair.

12. ___A___

13. We can have Robert reorganize the bookshelves—if you think it's needed—so that all the customer files will be together.

13. ___A___

14. Most visitors to Washington have one major stop in mind—the White House.

14. ___C___

15. Star Williams—to prove her point—found the letter within three minutes.

15. ___A___

(30 points)

Part C

two thirds of the country
three-fourths vote
self-assured
selfish
fifty-five
president-elect
reform the voter
thirty-three
my great-aunt Jane
two-fisted attitude

re-cover the sofa
well-behaved child
An *ad hoc* committee
a hit-or-miss approach
old-fashioned girl
double-spaced
fire-resistant material
resign the position
much-needed reforms
ex-president

Part D

1. The office needs one thing more—room.[21]

2. Christine Duvall, who is in charge of shipping, is an invaluable asset to the company; in other words, management has no intention of replacing her.

[21]This could also be punctuated: The office needs one thing more: room.

3. Three competing agencies—Jay Walker, Brown & Little, and Millers—are submitting bids on Thursday.

4. (One regular punctuation and one emphatic punctuation.) Joyce Andrews, much to everyone's surprise, has become an efficient manager—enviably efficient.

5. Payroll looked everywhere, so it was claimed, for my missing check; it was finally found behind the credenza.

6. Three fourths of our employees drive more than twenty minutes each way to work; unfortunately, we have no ride-sharing plan in effect.

7. (Punctuate in the regular way.) The following items are needed by Friday: a filled-in insurance form, a signed W-2 form, and two copies of your degree.

8. Reading your credentials, I find that you are exactly the person we have been looking for; can you start Monday?

9. The problem—the only problem that needs solving—is outlined in my report.

10. Our employees have never been accident-prone.

11. Today, not tomorrow, is our company's twenty-fifth anniversary.

12. That desk has serious problems—problems that our repairman has not even considered.

13. Are you applying for a part-time or full-time position?

14. Experience plus intelligence—that's the secret to success.

15. (Punctuate in the regular way.) This new plan must be cost-effective, or management will turn it down.

REVIEW EXERCISE #5

Part A   Score _____

1. A parenthetical statement that appears within the first of two clauses is punctuated as part of that clause.   1. __agree__

2. Never put a comma before an opening parenthesis.   2. __agree__

3. Parentheses are used to set off and de-emphasize.   3. __agree__

4. Brackets are only used within parentheses.   4. __disagree__

5. The word sic means "thus," and indicates that the author is being quoted exactly.   5. __agree__

6. Parentheses are used to enclose numbers or letters that identify items in series that appear in-line.

6. _agree_

7. Parenthetical expressions that are complete sentences are never punctuated as such.

7. _disagree_

8. Never put a mark of punctuation such as a question mark or an exclamation point within parentheses by itself.

8. _disagree_

9. Dollar amounts can be written out and placed in parentheses as arabic numbers plus dollar sign.

9. _agree_

10. Brackets can be used to inform the reader of added emphasis.

10. _agree_

(20 points)

Part B

1. To give added information at the end of a quotation.

1. _brackets_

2. To set off a parenthetical expression appearing in an introductory clause.

2. _parentheses_

3. To set off parenthetical expressions that are complete sentences.

3. _parentheses_

4. To substitute for parentheses when appearing inside existing parentheses.

4. _brackets_

5. To indicate bibliographic reference.

5. _brackets_

6. To enclose numbers or letters that identify items in a series or list written in-line.

6. _parentheses_

7. To de-emphasize a nonrestrictive phrase.

7. _parentheses_

8. To identify a mistake in a direct quotation.

8. _brackets_

9. To set off a single word as parenthetical.

9. _parenthesis_

10. To surround the word sic.

10. _brackets_

(20 points)

Part C

1. Our company manufactures radios, TV sets, refrigerators, and microwave ovens; and we are looking for ways to expand into other (more diversified?) fields.

2. The efficient receptionist, whether a man or a woman, is an undeniable asset to a company.[22]

3. Tact, wisdom, and courtesy—these are marks of the progressive manager.

4. The career-oriented college graduate is looking for a chance to break into a fast-growing, profitable, respected profession.

5. We have branch offices in Detroit, St. Louis, Cleveland, and New York at present; moreover, we are hoping to establish a London, England, branch by the end of the fiscal year.

6. A new firm (Career Inc.?) has just taken over the fifth floor of this building. (Uncertainty about the company name.)

7. The article stated "The losses to four brokerage house [sic] are currently estimated at over $4 million."

8. The markup for retailers, stores, banks, and mail order firms would be substantial; however, the projection assumes a complete sellout.

9. When we visited the Akron plant, we could not compare it with the home office plant.

10. Mr. Herring conducts most of his business by phone; however, he begins each morning by reading his mail.

11. The cufflinks are in the mail; you will notice (see the spring 1982 catalog) that we save you a substantial amount if you send in your order within five (5) days.

12. Your business, like any other new business, will benefit from experience.[23]

13. Some departments are experiencing high turnover; this department, however, has an excellent employee record.

14. Have your representative (Mr. Burn?) contact Mr. Feidler immediately.

15. The test was easy, wasn't it?

(60 points)

REVIEW EXERCISE #6

Part A   Score _____

1. Direct quotations are the exact words used by a writer or speaker.   1. _true_

2. Titles of major literary works usually appear in italics or are underlined.   2. _true_

[22]Non restrictive phrases and clauses can be set off by commas (first choice), dashes (for emphasis), or parentheses (to de-emphasize).

[23]This also has three acceptable ways.

3. Titles of movies are also in italics.
3. _false_

4. Periods and commas always appear inside the closing quotation mark.
4. _true_

5. Semicolons and colons always appear outside the closing quotation mark.
5. _true_

6. Short expressions are never used in an unconventional manner in this language.
6. _false_

7. A question mark, an exclamation mark, or a dash can appear either inside or outside a closing quotation mark.
7. _true_

8. Titles of minor works usually appear in quotation marks.
8. _true_

9. An indirect quotation is always set off by quotation marks.
9. _false_

10. Technical jargon or slang can be emphasized or clarified by the use of quotation marks.
10. _true_

(20 points)

Part B

Essays in Biography (Book)
   by John Maynard Keynes

The Wall Street Journal (Newspaper)

Fortune (Magazine)

Raiders of the Lost Ark (Movie)

Smithsonian (Magazine)

"Let It Be" (Song)
   by John Lennon

The Atlantic Monthly (Magazine)

The Affluent Society (Book)
   by John Kenneth Galbraith

"The Raven" (Poem)
   by Edgar Allen Poe

"Goodbye Columbus" (Short Story)
   by Phillip Roth

(20 points)

Part C

1. Mrs. Elliott asked, "Is organizational ability really important for a mid-management position?"

2. "Is organizational ability," asked Mrs. Elliott, "really important for a mid-management position?"

3. "Is organizational ability really important for a mid-management position?" asked Mrs. Elliott.

4. Was it Barbara McCauley who asked, "Is the Executive Club for men only?"

5. (Punctuate only the title Executive Club.) Was it Barbara McCauley who asked about the location of the "Executive Club"?

6. "Will you please make a copy of the article, 'Over-the-Counter Markets' in today's <u>Wall Street Journal</u>?" asked Robert Jones.

7. Roger interrupted us by saying, "Let me read you a quote from James C. Sanders, the new chief of the Small Business Administration, 'Few businesses can afford to borrow at current high interest rates.' "

8. Was it Barbara McCauley who asked if the Executive Club was for men only?

9. Did you see the article about the Small Business Association in the <u>Wall Street Journal</u>?

10. Look up the verb "savage" for me.

(20 points)

Part D

1. Writers frequently spell words from memory, but that spelling is often incorrect.

2. "To achieve success," said the general manager, "you must be willing to devote long difficult hours to learning your trade."

3. "There are features in this agreement, 'as it stands at present,' that are not satisfactory to the union," replied the business agent.

4. "Yes, gentlemen, business success is largely a matter of using what you have . . ." droned the general manager.

5. Do not accelerate the engine before it is warm; cold oil does not lubricate.[24]

6. "It is a pleasure to recommend Miss Paulo to anyone who is looking for a competent, obliging, and efficient stenographer," wrote Mr. Rogus.

7. If a court appearance is necessary, these terms will not apply; the fee will have to be arranged for in advance.

8. Our statements are based on exact knowledge, not vague hopes.

9. Any firm offering information plus service is bound to succeed, isn't it?

10. Lyle Holmes founded this company with only $1,000 and a dream (see page 20), and its success came slowly.

(40 points)

---

[24]Two independent clauses can be joined by a dash, instead of a semi-colon, if the second clause is to be emphasized.

REVIEW EXERCISE #7

Part A

1. you are ____you're____
2. 1937____'37____
3. do not ____don't____
4. 11 feet, 2 inches ____11'2"____
5. of the clock ____o'clock____

6. would not ____wouldn't____
7. 5 minutes, 30 seconds ____5'30"____
8. 1962 ____'62____
9. have not ____haven't____
10. who is ____who's____

(20 points)

Part B

1. The daughter of my boss.   my boss's daughter
2. The notes of the typists   the typists' notes
3. The statement of the vice-president   the vice-president's statement
4. The children of my brothers-in-law   my brothers-in-law's children
5. The finances of the firm   the firm's finances
6. The meeting of the directors   the directors' meeting
7. The suits of the men   the men's suits
8. The editorial in the <u>Los Angeles Times</u>   the Los Angeles Times' editorial
9. The policy of R. W. Murphy   R. W. Murphy's policy
10. The report of the committee   the committee's report
11. A delay of a month   a month's delay
12. The home of Susan and George   Susan and George's home
13. The sale of Henchey, Inc.   Henchey, Inc.'s, sale
14. The families of John and Frank   John's and Frank's families
15. The project of four weeks   four weeks' project

Part C

1. Tell Mr. Smith (<u>whose</u>, who's) program is more feasible, mine or (<u>hers</u>, her's).
2. (Its, <u>It's</u>) going to be a long meeting.

3. The messengers have been here and (there, <u>they're</u>, their) certain the packages are (<u>theirs</u>, their's, theres, there's).

4. Close the letter: (<u>Yours</u>, Your's) truly.

5. (<u>His</u>, His') report is extremely clear in (<u>its</u>, it's) presentation of the facts.

6. A representative of (our's, <u>ours</u>) is arranging for (they're, <u>their</u>) merger.

7. Good government is (everyones, everyones', <u>everyone's</u>) concern and depends on (everybodys, everybodys', <u>everybody's</u>) cooperation and support.

8. Jack Selby, (<u>whose</u>, who's) assignment includes programming the computer, wants to become a systems analyst eventually.

9. The personnel department is dedicated to work on (your're, <u>your</u>) behalf and (my, <u>mine</u>).

10. (Whose, <u>Who's</u>) the young woman in charge of accounts payable?

11. When the new IBM Selectric will be delivered is (anybodies, <u>anybody's</u>) guess.

12. We have sent the branch managers (our's, <u>ours</u>); however, some of the managers are slow in sending us (<u>theirs</u>, they'res, their's).

13. We owe a vote of gratitude to (<u>our</u>, our's) panel of experts for (<u>its</u>, it's) excellent presentation.

14. All employees are eligible for a 20 percent discount on the price of (they're, <u>their</u>) tickets.

15. (Were, <u>We're</u>) the management team responsible for (<u>this</u>, these) project.

(30 points)

Part D

1. The newspaper's point of view, which I do not share, is that a secretary's contribution most often exceeds an employer's.[25]

2. We asked Jerry's opinion, but he refused to discuss Susan's proposal.

3. The managers (was it at last Wednesday's meeting?) finally agreed to build an employees' recreation hall.

---

[25]There are three ways to punctuate the nonrestrictive clause: dashes, parentheses, or commas.

4. The AAA's vehicle license policy is designed to help with a new owner's registration.

5. The union has two weeks' time to accept or reject management's offer, but I believe the union's trouble has just begun.[26]

6. Yesterday's outmoded manufacturing techniques are not geared for today's needs; a concept that seems beyond management's understanding.

7. The foreman's view was that drastic changes had to be made in John's outlook if there was going to be any improvement.

8. The Reliance's policies are strictly under the ICC's direction.

9. If Miller and Miller's policy does not change, they will soon find themselves without clients to represent.

10. Frances' shop handles a complete line of women's ready-to-wear.

(20 points)

REVIEW EXERCISE #8

Part A   Score _____

1. 14 fourteenth
2. 77 seventy-seventh
3. 12 twelfth
4. 49 forty-ninth
5. 86 eighty-sixth
6. 72 seventy-second
7. 21 twenty-first
8. 43 forty-third
9. 35 thirty-fifth
10. 27 twenty-seventh

(20 points)

Part B

1. Arabic figures can begin sentences.   1. __D__

2. Expressing numbers as words tends to de-emphasize the number.   2. __A__

3. Spell out isolated numbers from one to ten.   3. __A__

---

[26]This is really a compound/complex sentence with an unvoiced noun clause functioning as a direct object: The union has two weeks time to accept or reject management's offer, but I believe (that) the union's trouble has just begun.

4. Spell out all ordinal numbers.

5. Spelling out isolated round numbers such as million or billion makes reading easier.

6. Arabic figures are used to express most exact numbers above ten.

7. Consistency is necessary when expressing numbers in words or Arabic figures.

8. The time of day should always be written out in words.

9. Identification numbers are expressed and punctuated in the same manner as count numbers.

10. Percentages are presented in Arabic figures with the word percent spelled out.

11. Write out the shorter of two consecutive numbers if no punctuation mark intervenes.

12. When two numbers occur together and both are either words or Arabic figures, separate them with commas.

13. Use commas in whole count numbers of four or more digits.

14. Never spell out indefinite numbers.

15. Arabic figure expression is used for emphasis.

4. _D_

5. _A_

6. _A_

7. _A_

8. _D_

9. _D_

10. _A_

11. _A_

12. _A_

13. _A_

14. _D_

15. _A_

(30 points)

Part C

1. If I'm not there by 7 o'clock, turn the extra 4 tickets back into the box office and credit my name.

1. seven four

2. The $.69 yellow pad now sells for $.98.

2. 69-cent 98 cents

3. Our new vice-president is only about 40 years old, but he has been with this company going on his 15th year.[27]

3. forty fifteenth

4. John Smothers will be attending a seminar tomorrow from 9:00 A.M. until 2:30 P.M.

4. _C_

5. The new secretary will be here at 9 o'clock on the 5 of next month.[28]

5. nine fifth

[27]15th is optional here.
[28]Optional: 5th

158

6. 2,000 or more people voted in the 21 District.[29]

    6. <u>two thousand twenty-first</u>

7. The pamphlet we have been working on for over 6 weeks will not be ready for another 5 days.

    7. <u>six five</u>

8. Where did you store the 17 69-cent envelopes and the 45 5-cent stamps that I purchased yesterday?

    8. <u>seventeen five-cent</u>

9. I interviewed 14 engineers, 7 programmers, and 22 cost accounts on a recent 5-day recruiting trip.

    9. <u>five-day</u>

10. The new security guard stands six feet seven inches tall and weighs two hundred twenty-five pounds.[30]

    10. <u>6 feet 7 inch 225 pounds</u>

11. Many of the applicants had difficulty in adding 3 1/4, one half, and two thirds.

    11. <u>1/2, 2/3</u>

12. The new Selectric typewriter weighs only 9 pounds and is fully guaranteed for 2 years.

    12. <u>nine two</u>

13. The magazine contains over one hundred suggestions for improving safety standards over a 5-state area.[31]

    13. <u>five-state</u>

14. We have not talked to Mr. Smith since the 3 of April, and we have over fifty new orders to place with him.[32]

    14 <u>third 50</u>

15. The records indicate that John paid $49.72 for his hotel room, $90 for meals, and $18.75 for telephone calls.

    15. <u>$90.00</u>

16. Sander J. Caldwell has made over $1,000,000 in insurance.

    16. <u>one million</u>

17. The plane, Western Flight seventy-two, leaves for Seattle at six forty-two P.M.

    17. <u>72 6:42 p.m.</u>

18. Our offices close promptly at 5:30 P.M. during the winter months and at 4:40 P.M. during the summer months.

    18. <u>C</u>

19. Even if you have as few as 5 phones, you can take advantage of the Executive electronic system.

    19. <u>five</u>

20. The corporate library has over 27 business management and business communications books in its five branch offices.

    20. <u>C</u>

[29]Optional: More than 2,000 people voted in the 21st District.
[30]Optional: 6' 7"; 225 lbs. (Considered very informal)
[31]Optional: 100 suggestions.
[32]Optional: 3rd of April or April 3.

159

21. Your check for <u>one thousand two hundred five dollars</u> arrived on <u>May 21st</u>.

21. $1,205
May 21

22. The board meeting lasted from <u>one-thirty</u> till five P.M.

22. 1:30
5:00

23. <u>1/2</u> of the positions in our San Diego office are filled by people with <u>5</u> years' experience.

23. one half
five

24. We have a scheduled meeting with five union representatives at 9:30 tomorrow morning.

24. C

25. Whereas a product may take from <u>six</u> to <u>36</u> months in design, its actual success is evident within <u>3</u> months of being on the market.

25. 6

(50 points)

REVIEW EXERCISE #9

Part A

Score_____

COMMON NOUN	PROPER NOUN	PROPER ADJECTIVE	PROPER ABBREVIATION OR NICKNAME
country	England	English	Engl.
city	New York	New Yorker	Big Apple
state	Georgia	Georgian	GA
man	Abraham Lincoln	Lincolnian	Honest Abe
doctor	Doctor of Philosophy	Doctoral	Ph.D.

Part B

1. <u>t</u>he <u>m</u>issouri and <u>m</u>ississippi rivers flow from North to south; the <u>o</u>hio <u>r</u>iver flows from east to west.

1. 6

2. The <u>S</u>outhern part of <u>t</u>exas, where I was born, is hottest during the summer.

2. 2

160

3. Mrs. Mitchell, the department supervisor of Jacobs Department Store spoke at the board of directors' meeting yesterday.

3. ___0___

4. The Director of the Lakeland hotel is john Golis jr., the Assistant director is still Marion Freeman.

4. ___5___

5. Every person of spanish descent should know that south america is represented at the united Nations.

5. ___4___

6. Our Attorney, Mr. anthony d. dowling, jr., assured us of our Rights against the Alliance insurance company.

6. ___8___

7. The Medlock tool co. appreciates the information received from the Corpus Christi board of Education on January 17.

7. ___3___

8. The southern California Advertising Agency of Bemis, Bormer, and Beard offers exceptional opportunities for Employment as far South as San Diego.

8. ___5___

9. The president left the white house by Helicopter at Noon and arrived at camp david within the Hour.

9. ___8___

10. The Point, a Motel/Hotel in phoenix, Arizona, offers tennis Courts, a String of fine saddle horses, and an excellent Golf Course for guests.

10. ___7___

11. Why don't you travel to san Francisco up Scenic highway 1 instead of going through the monterey peninsula?

11. ___5___

12. The Hotel where we like to stay in Carmel is of moorish design with wide spanish balconies.

12. ___3___

13. His Resumé indicates that his four years in High School and his two years in Community College were supported by part-time work at sears.

13. ___6___

14. As an Aid to our Dealers, we have arranged a tour at our factory on june 9 and 10.

14. ___3___

15. A Savings Account, however, draws exceptional Interest Rates at santa monica bank if a deposit is made before the 15th of each Month.

15. ___8___

REVIEW EXERCISE #10

Part A

1. Martin will be responsible for the following: books, tests, and brochures.
   Martin will be responsible for the following:
   1. Books
   2. Tests
   3. Brochures

2. The company has branch offices in the following states: Texas, Oklahoma, Arizona, and Nevada.
   The company has branch offices in the following states:
   A. Texas
   B. Oklahoma
   C. Arizona
   D. Nevada

3. Each desk should have certain supplies: manuscript paper, typewriter ribbons, and correction fluid.
   Each desk should have certain supplies:
   1. Manuscript paper
   2. Typewriter ribbons
   3. Correction fluid

4. Will you please submit the report in the usual manner: typed, double-spaced, summarized, and indexed.
   Will you please submit the report in the usual manner:
   A. Typed
   B. Double-spaced
   C. Summarized
   D. Indexed

(20 points)

Part B

Will you please go home now.
Will you please go home now!
Will you please go home now?

You know the answer.
You know the answer!
You know the answer?

You will be there.
You will be there!
You will be there?

The report was a success.
The report was a success!
The report was a success?

(20 points)

162

Part C

1. **AMA** American Medical Association
2. **CIA** Central Intelligence Agency
3. **FBI** Federal Bureau of Investigation
4. **IBM** International Business Machines
5. **NASA** National Aeronautics and Space Administration
6. **RN** Registered Nurse
7. **IOU** I owe you
8. **WP** Word processing
9. **TV** Television
10. **VIP** very important person
11. **Messrs** plural of Mr.
12. **NB** nota bene (mark well)
13. **rd.** road
14. **secy** secretary
15. **approx.** approximately
16. **BS** bill of sale
17. **Corp.** corporation
18. **dft.** draft
19. **expy.** expressway
20. **in.** inch(s)

(20 points)

Part D

1. How many policies did you sell in August? in September? in October?
2. Did you learn FORTRAN first?
3. Ouch! Try to be more careful.
4. (A Question) You are sure, Shirley, that you filed the papers?
5. Our new building is located at the corner of Olympic Blvd. and National Ave.
6. The average family in L.A. is spending over 37.7 percent of its income on housing.[33]

[33]Optional: LA; however, since this is so close to being a word, it is recommended that the periods be used to avoid confusion.

7. Will you please sign the enclosed voucher and return it to our office within the next three days.

8. Is he still the No. 1 salesman at Haley, Inc.

9. One of our underwriters (was it Martin?) wrote you concerning cancellation of the bond.

10. The sale offers savings ranging from $10.99 to $599.00 on floor samples.

11. If he were a member of the California AAA, he would enjoy the benefit of on-the-road repair service.[34]

12. What a stirring rendition of the "1812 Overture"!

13. Have you ever used the abbreviation i.e.?

14. H.R. Sellers, Inc., had a very good year in 1979.

15. Will you please mail this letter immediately.

16. More than 12.7 percent of the office staff had the flu in February.

17. Has the manager approved your suggestion "All personnel changes must be in writing"?

18. (An Exclamation) That was a long hike!

19. He asked if J.L. Stevens could work overtime this weekend.

20. Sure, he did.

(40 points)

March 5, 1982

Randall and Randall, Inc.
37 Tailor Avenue
Englewood Cliffs, New Jersey 07632

Gentlemen:

Janet deserves the highest rating for both her scholarly and creative ability. As a student in my class, Business English 207, she has contributed significantly to the improved attitude of many of her peers; she has always appeared totally involved in the subject matter, letter writing and she has created enthusiasm for the understanding of the communication process.

I feel extremely fortunate to have known Janet as both a student and, I believe, a friend. After only a short time in the class, I became aware of Janet's depth of knowledge where appreciation of English is concerned. This is particularly impressive, since English is not her first language.

[34]Optional: A.A.A.

Janet's good humor, zest, and careful preparation contribute to her classroom presence and make knowing her a pleasure. She upholds her end of an agreement, is aware of the details that make things work, and is a delightful person to meet.

Sincerely yours,

January 14, 1982

Medical Planning Association
18750 Wilshire Blvd.
Santa Monica, California 90401

Medical Planning Associates:

I am replying to your advertisement for a librarian/researcher/RN in the June 6, 1982, edition of the <u>Los Angeles Times</u>.

I am a registered nurse who will be graduating from a secretarial program at the end of June. I am planning to make a career change; however, I would consider utilizing my nursing background. My experience includes office, industrial, and hospital nursing.

Enclosed is a resumé that shows I do have many of the qualifications that you are seeking. Although I do not have any computer skills, I would be eager to learn.

I would be interested in an interview to discuss how my background may relate to your needs.

Yours truly,

March 15, 1983

Mr. Dennis Ely
Loyalty Finance Company
1219 Bule Crest Drive
Tampa, Florida 33614

Dear Mr. Ely:

Congratulations on your opening in Tampa last week.

We have the one hundred fifty (150) pounds of Hammermill bond paper in stock. We would be happy to print your logo on the paper with the royal blue ink you specified, if you like. The royal blue ink on the Hammermill bond is quite impressive; you've made an excellent choice.

As we have printed on the interior of the cover page of the catalog you ordered from, we have stringent credit requirements because of the volume of mail-order business we do. One of our requirements is that the firms to which we extend credit need to have been in business at their current address for at least one calendar year before becoming eligible.

We will be happy to complete processing your order if you care to send us cash, check, or money order. If you prefer, you can call your payment in by using any nationally recognized credit card.

Best wishes for a prosperous and successful year, and please feel free to reapply next year.

Sincerely yours,

December 13, 1982

Mr. Owen M. Peck
Peck & Peck, Inc.
627 Manchester Ave.
Anaheim, California 92802

Dear Mr. Peck:

Thank you for your letter of November 28 with enclosures.

Your comment that CPA-prepared statements would be forthcoming was most welcome, as a review of the current file information makes it apparent that our present case is a people case, plus three Nubian goats. This is the first time I have ever bonded three Nubian goats or, for that matter, even one Nubian goat; but I have admired the breed from afar for years and have always thought the prospect breathless.

I seem to be a bit short of background detail on the principals (the Jacksons, that is, not the goats); and I would appreciate having the enclosed contractor's questionnaire filled out so that we may fill in some of the gaps.

You mentioned in your letter that you had steered the Jacksons to their bank, and I think that is an excellent idea. I have a most entertaining mental image of them in conference with their loan officer, accompanied by their three Nubian goats.

It might also be wise to discuss their life insurance program. I wonder if your life insurance associate has ever ordered a physical on a Nubian goat.

Regards,

Part I

1. Shelly Adkins, my new manager, is from the Pacific North-west.
   - A. An abbreviation that follows a name
   - B. An "of phrase" that follows a name
   - √C. A nonrestrictive appositive

2. Gee, Tom seemed upset.
   - A. An adverb clause
   - √B. An interjection
   - C. A prepositional phrase

3. These shoes on display, Mrs. Jones, are the last pair on sale.
   - √A. A noun in direct address
   - B. Expresses a parenthetical thought
   - C. Interrupts the flow

4. In the fall, sale items are available.
   - A. Clauses built on contrast
   - √B. Easily misread words
   - C. Identification purposes

5. The monthly sales meeting will be held on Wednesday, not Friday.
   - √A. Contrasting expression
   - B. Omission of important words
   - C. Questions appended to statements

6. On the other hand, new materials are arriving daily.
   - A. Adverb clause
   - √B. Transitional phrase
   - C. Verbal phrase

7. Terry Kreutzer is an assertive, self-reliant young executive.
   - A. Words in a series
   - B. Clauses in a series
   - √C. Coordinate adjectives

8. The Sanfran Corporation, of Texas, has just opened new offices in Century City.
   - √A. An "of-phrase" that follows a name
   - B. An abbreviation that follows a name
   - C. A nonrestrictive appositive

9. To assure quality control, Tom checked each order person-ally.
   - A. Adverb clause
   - √B. Verbal phrase
   - C. Prepositional phrase

10. Ms. Ellen, obviously disturbed by the news, decided to go home early.

A. A noun in direct address
B. An adverb clause
√ C. Interrupts the flow

11. More than 1,483 delegates attended the conference.
    A. Easily misread words
    √ B. Number separation
    C. Identification purposes

12. The reasons for promptness and courtesy are self-evident, are they not?
    A. Contrasting expressions
    √ B. Questions appended to statements
    C. Omission of important words

13. The new manager strolled into the typing room, paused by the supervisor's desk, and casually asked who was in charge.
    √ A. Phrases in a series
    B. Clauses in a series
    C. Coordinate adjectives

14. Although Steve Webber has his Ed.D. degree, he feels he must prove himself constantly.
    A. Verbal phrase
    B. Prepositional phrase
    √ C. Adverb clause

15. The company has been managed by Jerry Scott, Ph.D., and Thelma Tolbert, M.A., for the past three years.
    √ A. An abbreviation that follows the name
    B. An "of-phrase" that follows the name
    C. A nonrestrictive appositive

16. The story having already been told, progress seemed relatively slow.
    A. Adverb clause
    B. Verbal phrase
    √ C. Nominative absolute

17. The new manager, however, seemed quite relieved by the news.
    A. Interrupts the flow.
    √ B. Expresses a parenthetical thought
    C. Can be in direct address

18. The more I pressed the issue, the more negative Mr. Styles became.
    √ A. Clauses built on contrast
    B. Number separation
    C. Easily misread words

19. Mrs. Stonewell's extension is 592, not 492.
    √ A. Contrasting expressions

168

B. Omission of important words
C. Chapter and page identification

20. In the case of severe storms, the plane will be grounded.
    A. Adverb clause
    B. Verbal phrase
    ✓ C. Prepositional phrase

21. Speed and accuracy can be increased by determination, practice, and hard work.
    A. Phrases in a series
    ✓ B. Words in a series
    C. Clauses in a series

22. Our original investment, a very substantial sum, has shown a creditable profit.
    ✓ A. A nonrestrictive appositive
    B. An "of-phrase" that follows a name
    C. A abbreviation that follows a name

23. As the manager walked into the room, he knew something was wrong.
    ✓ A. Adverb clause
    B. Transitional phrase
    C. Nominative absolute

24. Mr. Smith, can the decision be reversed?
    A. Interrupts the flow
    B. Expresses a parenthetical thought
    ✓ C. A noun in direct address

25. Did the sales manager ask, "Who made this sale?"
    A. Clauses built on contrast
    B. Easily misread words
    ✓ C. Identification purposes

Part II

26. To give added information to the reader, use
    ✓ A. Parentheses   B. Brackets

27. We need
    A. Two-thirds of the vote   ✓ B. Two thirds of the vote

28. He owns a
    ✓ A. 16-foot sailboat   B. 16 feet sailboat

29. It is now nine
    A. o clock   ✓ B. o'clock

30. I
    ✓ A. haven't decided yet   B. have'nt decided yet

31. To set off a parenthetical expression that is a complete sentence, use

√A. Parentheses   B. Brackets

32. To de-emphasize a nonrestrictive phrase, use

√A. Parentheses   B. Brackets

33. Next year I will turn

√A. forty-four   B. forty four

34. This will be a

√A. four-week project   B. four week's project

35. To surround the word <u>sic</u>, use

A. Parentheses   √B. Brackets

Part III

36. T   Titles of major literary works usually appear in italics or are underlined.

37. T   A semicolon is used to separate independent clauses not joined by a comma and a coordinate conjunction.

38. T   Identical verbs in a sentence are separated by commas.

39. F   Parenthetical expressions that are complete sentences are never punctuated as such.

40. T   Spell out isolated numbers from <u>one</u> to <u>ten</u>.

41. F   Spell out all ordinal numbers.

42. T   A question mark, an exclamation point, or a dash can appear inside or outside a closing quotation mark.

43. F   Introductory elements are usually followed by a semicolon.

44. T   Use commas to separate items in an address when that address is written <u>in-line</u>.

45. F   Never put a mark of punctuation such as a question mark or an exclamation point within parentheses by itself.

46. T   Write out the shorter of two consecutive numbers if no punctuation mark intervenes.

47. T   When two numbers occur together and both are either words or figures, separate them with commas.

48. F   An indirect quotation is always set off by quotation marks.

49. T   A conjunctive adverb is a description of the placement of a parenthetical adverb next to the semicolon joining two independent clauses.

50. T   Use commas to separate items in a date.

51. F   Brackets are only used within parentheses.

52. T   The word <u>sic</u> means "thus," and indicates that the author is being quoted exactly.

53. T   Parentheses are used to enclose numbers or letters that identify items that appear <u>in-line</u> in series.

54. T   Consistency is necessary when expressing numbers in words or figures.

55. T   A colon is used after a formal introduction that includes or suggests words such as <u>the following</u>.

56. T   Expressions that begin with <u>not</u>, <u>never</u>, or <u>seldom</u> are set off by commas.

57. T   Periods and commas always appear inside the closing quotation mark.

58. T   Semicolons and colons always appear outside the closing quotation mark.

59. T   In some cases a semicolon can be a mark of elevation.

60. F   A colon is never used to separate two main clauses.

Part IV

61. B   (A) 40, (B) Forty, (C) Fourty leading production engineers visited the plant last week.

62. C   Good government is (A) everyones, (B) everyones', (C) everyone's concern.

63. B   The deliverymen have been here and (A) there, (B) they're, (C) their certain that the mistake has been corrected.

64. A   We owe a vote of gratitude to (A) our, (B) hour, (C) our's panel of experts.

65. C   (A) Your, (B) Your's, (C) You're truly an asset to the company.

66. C   All employees are eligible for a 20 percent discount on the price of (A) they're, (B) there, (C) their season tickets.

67. A   Jack Selby, (A) whose, (B) whos, (C) who's office this is, has agreed to the merger.

68. B   The package is (A) theres, (B) theirs, (C) their's.

69. B   Close the letter: (A) <u>your's</u> (B) <u>Yours</u>, (C) <u>yours truly</u>.

70. A   This report is extremely clear in (A) its, (B) it's, (C) its' presentation of the facts.

Part V

71.   A.   These courses are required of all computer majors namely physics, math, and statistics.
   √ B.   These courses are required of all computer majors; namely, physics, math, and statistics.
   C.   These courses are required of all computer majors, namely, physics, math, and statistics.

72. √ A.   The Southern California advertising agency of Bemis, Bormer, and Beard offers exceptional opportunities for employment as far south as San Diego.
   B.   The southern California Advertising Agency of Bemis, Bormer, and Beard: offers exceptional opportunities for Employment as far south as San Diego.
   √ C.   The Southern California Advertising Agency of Bemis, Bormer, and Beard offers exceptional opportunities for Employment as far south as San Diego.

73.   A.   When we saw the movie Ragtime we did not compare it with the book Ragtime by Doctorow.
   B.   When we saw the movie "Ragtime," we did not compare it with the book Ragtime by Doctorow.
   √ C.   When we saw the movie Ragtime, we did not compare it with the book Ragtime by Doctorow.

74.   A.   The new training class is 3/4 full.
   √ B.   The new training class is three-fourths full.
   C.   The new training class is three fourths full.

75. √ A.   Debbie frequently spells until with two l's, but that spelling is incorrect.
   B.   Debbie frequently spells until with two ls but that spelling is incorrect.
   C.   Debbie frequently spells until with two ls, but that spelling is incorrect.

76.   A.   This building is scheduled for demolition beginning June 15 the new building moreover is not scheduled for completion until June 1985.
   √ B.   This building is scheduled for demolition beginning June 15; the new building, moreover, is not scheduled for completion until June 1985.
   C.   This building is scheduled for demolition beginning June 15 the new building; moreover, is not scheduled for completion until June 1985.

77.   A.   Three competing agencies Jay Walker Brown & Little and Millers are submitting bids Thursday.

    ✓ B.   Three competing agencies—Jay Walker, Brown & Little, and Millers—are submitting bids Thursday.

    C.   Three competing agencies (Jay Walker Brown & Little and Millers) are submitting bids Thursday.

78. ✓ A.   One half of the positions in our San Diego office are filled by people with five years' experience.

    B.   1/2 of the positions in our San Diego office are filled by people with 5 years experience.

    C.   One-half of the positions in our San Diego office are filled by people with 5 years experience.

79. A.   The article stated The losses to four brokerage house sic are currently estimated at over $4 million.

    B.   The article stated, "The losses to four brokerage house sic are currently estimated at over $4,000,000."

    ✓ C.   The article stated, "The losses to four brokerage house [sic] are currently estimated at over $4 million."

80. A.   The Medlock tool co.; appreciates the information received from the Corpus Christi board of Education on January 17.

    ✓ B.   The Medlock Tool Co. appreciates the information received from the Corpus Christi Board of Education on January 17.

    C.   The Medlock Tool Co. appreciates the information received from the Corpus Christi Board of Education on January 17.

81. A.   Sander J Caldwell has made over $1,000,000 in insurance.

    ✓ B.   Sander J. Caldwell has made over a million dollars in insurance.

    C.   Sander J. Caldwell has made over $1,000,000 in insurance.

82. A.   He is still the No. 1 salesman at Haley, Inc..

    B.   Is he still the No. 1 salesman at Haley Inc

    ✓ C.   He is still the No. 1 salesman at Haley, Inc.

83. A.   John was granted a 2 month leave.

    ✓ B.   John was granted a two-month leave.

    C.   John was granted a 2-month leave.

84. ✓ A.   Why don't you travel along the coast up scenic Highway 1 to San Francisco?

    B.   Why don't you travel to San Francisco; up scenic Highway 1, along the coast?

    C.   Why don't you travel to san Francisco up Scenic highway 1: along the coast.

85. A. Three fourths of our employees drive more than twenty minutes each way to work unfortunately we have no ride-sharing plan in effect.

B. Three-fourths of our employees drive more than twenty minutes each way to work, unfortunately; we have no ride-sharing plan in effect.

✓ C. Three fourths of our employees drive more than twenty minutes each way to work; unfortunately, we have no ride-sharing plan in effect.

86. A. Was it Barbara McCauley who asked, "if the Executive club was for men only"?

✓ B. Was it Barbara McCauley who asked if the Executive Club was for men only?

C. Was it Barbara McCauley who asked" if the Executive Club was for men only?"

87. A. The managers was it at last Wednesday meeting? finally agreed to build an employees recreation hall.

✓ B. The managers (was it at last Wednesday's meeting?) finally agreed to build an employees' recreation hall.

C. The managers, was it at last Wednesdays meeting; finally agreed to build an employees recreation hall.

88. ✓ A. We are presently editing 5 technical manuals, 42 company handouts, and 17 brochures

B. We are presently editing five technical manuals, 42 company handouts, and 17 brochures.

C. We are presently Editing five technical manuals, forty-two company handouts, and 17 brochures.

89. A. His resumé indicates that his four years in High School; and his two years in Community College were supported by part-time work at sears.

✓ B. His resumé indicates that his four years in high school and his two years in community college were supported by part-time work at Sears.

C. His resumé indicates that his four years in High school and his two years in Community college were supported by Part-time work at Sears.

90. ✓ A. Most visitors to Washington have one major stop in mind: the White House.

B. Most visitors to Washington have one Major Stop in mind: the White House.

C. Most Visitors to Washington have one major stop in mind; the White House.

91. A. The Director of the Lakeland hotel is john Golis; jr.; the Assistant director is still Marion Freeman.

B. The Director of the Lakeland Hotel is John Golis, jr., the Assistant director is still Marion Freeman.

✓ C. The director of the Lakeland Hotel is John Golis, Jr.; the assistant director is still Marion Freeman.

92. A. We have in stock at this writing the following sizes A-9613 H9472 and J8923.

✓ B. We have in stock, at this writing, the following sizes: A-9613, H-9472, and J-9823.

C. We have in stock at this writing the following sizes; A9,613, H9,472, and J9,823.

93. ✓ A. Reading your credentials, I find that you are exactly the person we have been looking for; can you start Monday?

B. Reading your credentials I find thay you are exactly the person we have been looking for can you start Monday?

C. Reading your credentials; I find thay you are exactly the person we have been looking for. Can you start Monday?

94. A. Is organizational ability really important for a mid-management position? asked Mrs. Elliott.

B. Is organizational ability really Important for a Mid-management position asked Mrs. Elliott.

✓ C. "Is organizational ability really important for a mid-management position?" asked Mrs. Elliott.

95. A. The newpapers point of view which I do not share is that a secretarys contribution most often exceeds an employers.

✓ B. The newspaper's point of view (which I do not share) is that a secretary's contribution most often exceeds an employer's.

C. The Newspapers' point of view (which I do not share) is that a secretarys' contribution most often exceeds an employers.

96. A. The sales tax on this item amounts to one dollar, and thirty two cents.

B. The sales tax on this item amount to one dollar and thirty-two cents.

✓ C. The sales tax on this item amounts to $1.32.

97. ✓ A. Roger interrupted us by saying, "Let me read you a quote from James C. Sanders, the new chief of the Small Business Administration, 'Few businesses can afford to borrow at current high interest rates.'"

B. Roger interrupted us by saying Let me read you a quote from James C. Sanders the new chief of the

175

Small Business Administration Few businesses can afford to borrow at current high interest rates.

   C.   Roger interrupted us by saying, "Let me read you a quote from James C. Sanders, the new chief of the Small Business Administration Few businesses can afford to borrow at current high interest rates."

98.   A.   A Savings Account; however, draws exceptional Interest Rates at santa monica band if a deposit is made before the 15th of each month.

  √ B.   A savings account, however, draws exceptional interest rates at Santa Monica Bank if a deposit is made before the 15th of each month.

   C.   A Savings Account, however; draws exceptional interest rates at Santa Monica bank if a deposit is made before the 15th of each month.

99.   A.   The missouri and mississippi rivers flow from North to south, the ohio river flows from east to west.

  √ B.   The Missouri and Mississippi rivers flow from north to south; the Ohio River flows from east to west.

   C.   The Missouri and Mississippi Rivers flow from North to South: the Ohio River flows from East to West.

100. √ A.   If Miller & Miller's policy does not change, it will soon find itself without clients to represent.

   B.   If Miller and Millers policy does not change they will soon find themselves without clients to represent.

   C.   If Miller & Miller's policy does not change; it will soon find itself without clients' to represent.

DIAGNOSTIC TEST

Commas

1. Johnson is a responsible, fair-minded manager.
2. In adding the receipts, Fred made a serious mistake.
3. If you have any questions, Ms. Smith, the personnel department bulletin may be able to answer them.
4. The credit union will stay open late on Wednesday, Thursday, and Friday of next week.
5. Mr. Hickson carefully locked the safe, but he forgot the combination.
6. Mrs. Tyson, on the other hand, never forgets a thing.
7. The company does not withhold federal or state income taxes from your checks.

8. The first speaker is Thomas B. Redding, Ph.D., and he will keynote the conference on Thursday morning.

Semicolons and Colons

9. Tom Simmons simply quoted the closing figures; he did not comment on their validity.

10. Our company is initiating a new four-day week; however, the participation is flexible and begins at 6:30 A.M.

11. The conference has been held in Denver, Colorado; Palm Springs, California; and Salt Lake City, Utah.

12. The following names were on the promotion list; namely, Elliot James, Valerie Drummond, and Kent Butler.

13. These names were left out of the recent telephone directory; please add them to your list.

14. The people in accounting will be working Saturdays for the whole month; furthermore, the people in accounts receivable will be working overtime next month.

15. Mr. Kelly will attend all the meetings; Ms. Ward, on the other hand, will only attend the first meeting.

Dashes, Parentheses, and Hyphens

16. There is only one thing on John Smother's mind—profit.

17. Hammers, nails, saws—these are the tools of the trade.

18. There were over thirty-three applicants for one position.

19. The answer to that question is in the management books (see Chapter 2, page 24).

20. John Doe hereby agrees to pay the undersigned four hundred and twenty-five dollars ($425).

21. Alec Parsons has lost the figures—figures that were needed to close the bid.

22. (Punctuate for emphasis) The three competing offices—San Mateo, Santa Rosa, and San Francisco—have been setting district sales records.

Quotation Marks

23. "The success of the company," said Mr. Allerton, "is due to the combined efforts of management and staff."

24. Did you hear Mr. Lopez say, "No one is willing to work hard any more"?

25. "There is only one area that will give you the opportunity to exercise your talent," said Dr. Jordan.

26. "When did you hear from him last?" asked the manager.

27. Mr. Browning, the district manager, used these exact words: "Be completely honest and success is inevitable."

28. "What is the new manager's name?" asked the foreman.

29. Doris Moore suggested, "Tom Ward had the right idea when he asked, 'What's in it for me?' during last Friday's staff meeting."

30. Seeing the approaching truck, Janice shouted, "Watch out!"

Apostrophes

31. Mr. Jones' talent for cost accounting can't be duplicated in this company.

32. The word <u>success</u> has two c's and two s's.

33. The Board of Directors' meeting has been postponed.

34. There will be five minutes' delay before the presentation begins.

35. The Wallaces' warehouse is on the next block; that warehouse is the Adamses'.

36. Tom and Dave's study is better than ours.

37. Did you hear about Hendly, Inc.'s, sale?

38. It's a pleasure when its gearshift works.

Numbers

39. Invoice No. <u>4,276</u> has been delayed for <u>3</u> days.

40. Approximately <u>two-thirds</u> of the vote went in our favor.

41. The final shipment will include <u>fourteen</u> desk blotters, 2 new Selectric typewriters, and 24 hand calculators.

42. Be sure to stay on Highway <u>Fifteen</u> for at least twenty-five minutes before looking for the exit.

43. <u>5</u> new accounts have added to the staff in the past <u>fifteen</u> days.

Capitalization

44. Please meet <u>mr.</u> <u>thompson</u> at his office <u>monday</u>.

45. The <u>A</u>udience enjoyed brunch on fine <u>C</u>hina after the morning <u>L</u>ecture.

46. We celebrate the signing of the declaration of independence on july 4 each year.

47. The Jones Brothers construction Company is remodeling both the Woolworth and the Smiley Buildings.

48. While in night School, i'm studying French and Shorthand.

49. While you're at the Drugstore, please pick up a box of Kleenex and a Bic Pen for me.

50. Last Wednesday, Mr. fox returned to Culver city.

Index